Extreme Fabulations

Extreme Fabulations

Science Fictions of Life

Steven Shaviro

Goldsmiths
Press

Copyright © 2021 Goldsmiths Press
First published in 2021 by Goldsmiths Press
Goldsmiths, University of London, New Cross
London SE14 6NW

Printed and bound by Versa Press
Distribution by the MIT Press
Cambridge, Massachusetts, and London, England

Copyright © 2021 Steven Shaviro

A CIP record for this book is available from the British Library

ISBN 978-1-912685-88-2 (hbk)
ISBN 978-1-912685-87-5 (ebk)

www.gold.ac.uk/goldsmiths-press

Goldsmiths
UNIVERSITY OF LONDON

For Adah and Roxanne, as always.
And in memory of Leo Daugherty and of Joseph Libertson.

Contents

Preface

This book was mostly written between 2017 and 2019, though some of the books I write about here were previously (and sketchily) discussed on my blog, *The Pinocchio Theory*. Versions of several chapters were presented as talks at the International Conference on the Fantastic in the Arts, the Science Fiction Research Association annual conferences, and the "Speculative Thinking in Literature and Philosophy" workshop at the Haus der Kulturen der Welt in Berlin.

Writing is a solitary endeavor, but it could not take place without a wide network of support. I would like especially to thank Roddey Reid, who gave me valuable feedback on the entire manuscript. Carol Vernallis also read and commented on many of these chapters. In addition, I am thankful for the encouragement and support I have received from many scholars in the science fiction research community. This is a connection that dates back some 45 years, to the time when I avidly discussed matters science fictional in graduate school with Carl Freedman, John Rieder, and Christopher Kendrick. More recently, I have benefited from scholarly exchanges with Mark Bould, Sherryl Vint, Rhys Williams, and many others. Outside of science fiction, Armen Avanessian provided support, as well as occasions for me to present my work.

I would also like to thank the science fiction writers themselves, whose works have been the occasions for my commentaries. Gilles Deleuze once said: "my ideal, when I write about an author, would be to write nothing that could cause him sadness, or if he is dead, that might make him weep in his grave." I have always tried to adhere to this standard, though of course it is not for me to say whether or not I have succeeded.

Thanks are also due to the band clipping., who graciously gave me permission to quote from the lyrics to their album *Splendor and Misery*.

I would also like to give recognition to my favorite cafe, Avalon International Breads in midtown Detroit, where large portions of this book were written.

This book has a double dedication. I would like to recall two great spirits, recently passed, whom I have long regarded as mentors: Leo Daugherty (died 2015) and Joseph Libertson (died 2020). But also, as always, this book is dedicated to my daughters, Adah and Roxanne, in the hope that the future world in which they outlive me will be a better place than our current one.

Introduction

This book is a thought experiment. It discusses a number of science fiction narratives: three novels, one novella, three short stories, and one musical concept album. The works in question date from 1950 to 2017. Each chapter stands on its own as an exercise in close and careful reading. But together, in sequence, these eight analyses pursue a single line of thought. *Extreme Fabulations* is concerned with life and embodiment. I start with questions of what Kant called the "conditions of possibility" for life and thought to be able to exist at all, and for human beings to confront the rest of the universe (Chapters 1 and 2). I then consider questions of how we understand life pragmatically, and how we may thereby imagine controlling and changing it (Chapters 3 and 4). From there, I move on to ask questions about the aesthetic and social dimensions of human existence, in relation to the nonhuman (Chapters 5 and 6). And finally, I grapple with questions about the ethical value of human life under conditions of extreme oppression and devastation (Chapters 7 and 8).

I pursue these questions neither philosophically nor scientifically, but through the medium of science fiction. I believe that science fiction writing, at its best, offers us a unique way of grappling with issues that deeply and unavoidably concern us, but that are intractable to rational argumentation or to empirical verification. This is not to deny the importance of abstract reasoning and of quantitative research, but merely to acknowledge, as John Maynard Keynes put it, that much of the time "we simply do not know" what is going to happen. The future is not closed. In a casino, we can mathematically assign probabilities to every possible outcome arising from the spin of a roulette wheel, or the shuffling of a pack of cards. High finance attempts to apply this casino logic to everything in the world. But as Keynes argued long ago, such an endeavor cannot succeed. For in the broader world, there is no such thing as a finite set of all possible outcomes, on the basis of which we could assign them relative probabilities.

Science fiction, despite what is sometimes said about it, does not really claim to predict the future. It is neither prophetic nor probabilistic. It is true that science fiction – like what the business world calls "strategic foresight" – extrapolates from actually existing trends and tendencies, and imagines what might happen in the future if they were to continue. It is also true that science fiction texts – like derivatives and other arcane financial instruments – speculate upon the contingent outcomes of uncontrolled and even unknowable processes. But beyond both of these, science fiction crucially involves a movement of fabulation. The future is unavoidably vague and multifarious; it stubbornly resists our efforts to know it in advance, let alone to guide it or circumscribe it. But science fiction takes up this very vagueness and indeterminacy, by rendering it into the form of a self-consciously fictional narrative. It gives us characters who experience the vagaries of unforeseeable change.

In other words, science fictional fabulation concretizes futurity as such, with its social, technological, and ontological indeterminacy intact. In this way, it does something similar to what Claude Lévi-Strauss defines as the function of myth: which is "to provide a logical model capable of overcoming a contradiction (an impossible achievement if, as it happens, the contradiction is real)" (Lévi-Strauss 1963). But Lévi-Strauss sees myths as synchronic structures, existing all at once, suspended in the eternal present of a given society. In contrast, narratives are in their very nature diachronic or temporal – or better, historical. Science fictional fabulation deals in futurity, rather than being set in the eternal present of myth. In this way, science fiction is counterfactual, or (to alter this too-familiar word) counter-actual: it offers us a provisional and impossible resolution, suspended in potentiality, of dilemmas and difficulties that are, themselves, all too real.

Henri Bergson, who introduced the notion of fabulation into philosophy, defines it as "a counterfeit of experience," or a "a systematically false experience," that nonetheless has considerable value, precisely because of the way that "it can thwart our judgment and reason."

Fabulation emerges in conditions of emergency; it works to preserve us from the dangers of excessive certainty, or of "pushing too far" with our rationalizations (Bergson 1935). In its vital urgency, science fiction exemplifies Alfred North Whitehead's maxim that "in the real world it is more important that a proposition be interesting than that it be true" (Whitehead 1978).

Insofar as it is a "counterfeit of experience" that suspends our usual assumptions and trains of thought, science fictional fabulation demands to be taken literally. That is to say, any successful work of science fiction produces a powerful reality-effect. We cannot take its descriptions only as allegories or metaphors. We also need to accept them as factual conditions that have unavoidably been given to us, at least within the frame of the narrative. By speaking of givenness, I am trying to suggest that – in the world of a science fictional work – these conditions both overtly display to us their contingency or arbitrariness, and yet at the same time stare us directly in the face with their ineluctable actuality.

In this book, I try to take the science fiction narratives that I examine as literally, and as fully, as possible. Of course such an endeavor can never entirely succeed. Any text, and any commentary, is unavoidably riddled with all sorts of unwanted distortions and presuppositions. Nonetheless, I hope that I have succeeded in tracing a meaningful trajectory through these eight works of extreme fabulation. Chapter 1 discusses "The New Reality," by Charles Harness, a short story that takes Kant's *Critique of Pure Reason* as its novum, or science fictional premise. This forces us to question the extent to which the real, external world can in fact be correlated with, or made to conform to, the all-too-human assumptions with which we approach it. Chapter 2, on Adam Roberts' novel *The Thing Itself*, continues this line of Kantian questioning, asking what it might mean to imagine stepping outside the anthropocentric framework. This leads to doubts both about how we understand life, and about what we might imagine as the lifeless void. Chapter 3, on Clifford Simak's short story "Shadow Show," follows on to look at changing conceptualizations of life, both in science fiction and in actual biological practice. Chapter 4, with its discussion of Ann

Halam's young adult novel *Dr. Franklin's Island*, extends these considerations in order to focus both on the scientific power to control life, and on the degree to which vital processes themselves may resist or push back against such control. Chapter 5 discusses Nalo Hopkinson's short story "Message in a Bottle" in order to look at the ways that life is manifested in the potentialities and limitations of artistic creation. The chapter, following the story, touches on questions of both biological and social reproduction, and of our ability to confront the open future. Chapter 6, on Chris Beckett's novel *Dark Eden*, moves these questions about vitality, reproduction, and futurity from an aesthetic register to an anthropological one. The last two chapters then work through all the concerns of the earlier sections in the context of our all-too-vivid experiences of social, economic, and political oppression. Chapter 7 looks at *Splendor and Misery*, a concept album by the experimental hip hop group clipping. Chapter 8 considers Gwyneth Jones' novella *Proof of Concept*. Both of these chapters raise the prospect of abolition or extinction: a flight into the unknown as an ethico-political alternative to the catastrophes inflicted by an unjust social order. This returns us to the cosmic perspective of the opening chapters, with their endeavors to come to terms with a universe not to the measure of human prejudices and desires.

Chapter 1

The New Reality

Charles L. Harness' 1950 short story "The New Reality" (Harness 1950) is about a scientific experiment that threatens to "destroy the Einsteinian universe." Adam Prentiss Rogers, the story's protagonist, is an "ontologist" working for the International Bureau of the Censor. His mission is to "keep reality as is," by suppressing any scientific research that might "alter the shape of that reality." But such research is actually being conducted by the story's antagonist, Professor Luce. He has invented "a practical device – an actual machine – for the wholesale alteration of incoming sensoria," the raw material of subjective experience. Once he runs this device, human beings will be bombarded with "novel sensoria" that "can't be conformed to our present apperception mass." That is to say, our minds will be traumatically overwhelmed by sensations that we are unable to process.

What can this mean? Kant famously warns us that "thoughts without content are empty, intuitions without concepts are blind." Luce's experiment threatens (and intends) to "blind" us, by producing "intuitions" (Kant's word for sensations) to which our usual concepts cannot be applied. Reality will no longer fit into the shapes that we impose upon it, and through which we are able to parse it. Faced with such disruption, experience as we know it will fall apart. "Instead of a [space-time] continuum, our 'reality' would become a disconnected melange of three-dimensional objects. Time, if it existed, wouldn't bear any relation to spatial things." The vast majority of humankind will not be able to navigate such a new reality. The only people able to "get through," to grasp the altered state of the world and function within it, will be "the two or three who understood advanced ontology": Prentiss,

Luce, and perhaps Prentiss' boss and love interest, the woman known only as E. In a classic display of scientific *hubris*, familiar from so many science fiction stories, Luce promises that the two or three of them "will be gods," finally able "to know all things" as they truly are.

One obvious way to take "The New Reality" is as an allegory of relentless scientific and technological progress. As George Zebrowski puts it, in his general introduction to Harness' work, the story "takes its strength from the dynamic fact of human scientific development, by which the growth of our knowledge is linked to new ideas and imaginings." For the last several centuries, new technologies have traumatically overwhelmed us, leaving us numb and alienated – a theme treated by such thinkers as Walter Benjamin and Marshall McLuhan. More specifically, "The New Reality" anticipates what later came to be called *future shock*: as in the 1970 book of that title by Alvin Toffler, and John Brunner's 1975 science fiction novel *The Shockwave Rider*. It is not for nothing that, in his day job, Harness was a patent lawyer; he was well positioned to see how the rapid pace of technological innovation might surpass our ability to adjust to it.

But "The New Reality" also warns us that the violent change it envisions is not just a matter of "something like the application of the quantum theory and relativity to the production of atomic energy, which of course has changed the shape of civilization." The disruption goes much further than this. Beyond the pragmatic "application" of scientific theories, we must consider the basic ontology of the scientific process itself. The story anticipates, by more than a decade, Thomas Kuhn's notion of paradigm shifts in the history of science (*The Structure of Scientific Revolutions*). In the course of what Kuhn calls *scientific revolutions*, new models of reality are introduced. These new models do not just reflect the accumulation of additional empirical data; they are often flatly incompatible with the prevailing previous ones. The Einsteinian universe is quite different from the Newtonian universe that it replaced. As Zebrowski notes, people have historically found it difficult to accept and adapt to such changes in our world picture as "the dethroning of the Earth as the center of the universe" (Copernicus) and the theory of "evolution by natural selection" (Darwin).

"The New Reality" radicalizes the drama of scientific paradigm change by the simple expedient of taking it naively – which is to say, literally. The story's basic premise is that our consensus reality is itself merely a historical construct. The physical universe has actually changed over the course of time, in tandem with the development of science. For instance, the story tells us that the world really was flat when people thought it was flat, prior to 500 BC; now it is actually round because our theories tell us that it must be. The "Late Greeks" inferred the spherical shape of the Earth from their observation "that [the] mast of [an] approaching ship appeared first, then [the] prow." But if "earlier seafaring peoples" like the Minoans never made this observation, it is because there was no such phenomenon for them to observe. We should not think that they failed to notice because "they worked with childish premises and infantile instruments." Rather, the Minoans were sophisticated in their own way; it is just that the curvature of the Earth didn't exist yet. In 1000 BC, the mast of a distant ship did not appear any earlier than the prow. Five hundred years later, the Late Greeks observed this phenomenon because their metaphysics required evidence of roundness, which the Minoans' earlier metaphysics had not.

Or, to give another example, today it is an established truth that the rocks making up the Earth's crust are millions or billions of years old. But the story suggests that this was not the case in the seventeenth century, when everyone *just knew* that the Earth itself was only six thousand years old. At that time, the best scientists "studied chalk, gravel, marble, and even coal, without finding anything inconsistent with results to be expected from the Noachian Flood." It was only during the course of the nineteenth century that these rocks retrospectively became much older. It's a bit like the *retcon* (retroactive continuity) process sometimes found in comics, and in fantasy and science fiction stories. For instance, in *Buffy the Vampire Slayer*, the character of Dawn is introduced at the start of the show's fifth season; but subsequently, everyone in the story remembers her as having been there from the beginning. In a similar way, the nineteenth century *needed* ancient rocks, because it had invented deep geological time; and so the antiquity of the rocks was established by scientific study.

"The New Reality" suggests, therefore, that the "apparent universe" is "the work of man," largely a product of "the omnipotent human mind." Again and again, we come up with "theory first, then we alter 'reality' to fit." Even at best, as Prentiss explains in the course of the story, reality *as we know it* is "nothing more than a working hypothesis in the mind of each of us, forever in a process of revision." And basic scientific research – at least in times of what Kuhn calls *revolutionary science* – involves such revision on a grand scale. Kuhn himself holds back from claiming that "when paradigms change, the world itself changes with them" – though he comes close. But "The New Reality" takes this final step, and argues that paradigm shifts determine and produce actual physical shifts. What "man" (sic) imagines to be the result of "a broadened application of science and more precise methods of investigation" is actually the sign and the consequence of "his own mental quickening."

"The New Reality" thus argues that we have largely made the world – or at least the "apparent" world – over in our own image. Science fiction commonly extrapolates from particular technological developments or social trends. But here, the extrapolation occurs on a meta-level. The story projects forward, not from any particular scientific innovation, but from the very fact that such innovation happens in the first place. Science is always revising our understanding of the world. One might be tempted to say, therefore, that "The New Reality" gives us a metaphor for scientific progress. But in fact, the story does the opposite of this. For it *literalizes* the metaphors that we generally use to describe the development of science. Indeed, at one point Prentiss explicitly denies that he is merely giving "a rhetorical description of scientific progress over the past centuries," as when someone says "that modern transportation and communications have shrunk the earth." Rather, Prentiss claims that our planet has *literally* changed from flat to round, and from relatively new to unimaginably ancient.

"The New Reality" justifies these outrageous claims by appealing to Kant's *Critique of Pure Reason*. As Professor Luce writes of Kant in his journal: "it seemed incredible that this silent little man, who had never been outside of Königsberg, should hold the key to the universe."

And yet the *Critique* does provide this key. Kant tells us that external reality takes the shape it does only because it necessarily conforms to our minds: which is to say, to the ways that we organize and categorize "incoming sensoria" (i.e., empirical sense-data). Perception is never raw or unmediated. It is always already processed, shaped, and conceptualized by us. Experience comes predigested, as it were. This means that we do not ever encounter things as they truly are in themselves (*noumena*), but only things as they appear to us, in the ways that they have been organized by our own powers of understanding (*phenomena*).

Of course, "The New Reality" extrapolates far beyond anything that Kant himself actually said, or would have agreed to. According to Kant, even though the structures that govern the phenomenal world are our own imposition, they are not merely arbitrary. If we find the universe embedded in relations of time and space, and organized according to processes like cause and effect, this is because these relations and processes are necessary forms of the human understanding, dictated by the structure of rationality itself. We cannot change these forms and categories. We lack the ability to see things otherwise; cognition cannot work any other way.

But the story pushes relentlessly beyond these limits. As Professor Luce also remarks, despite Kant's genius: "I doubt that even he realizes the ultimate portent of his teaching." This "ultimate portent" is attained by radically *historicizing* Kant's argument. This means transforming Kant's necessary conditions into something like multiple, incommensurable Kuhnian paradigms; or like the different *epistemes* (*a priori* structures of understanding) that Michel Foucault posits for different social and historical periods (*The Order of Things*). "The New Reality" posits that our *a priori* assumptions have themselves evolved over the course of human history, as our minds have grown and changed. We find ourselves retrospectively rewriting both human history and natural history, because this is the only way to guarantee that phenomena will continue to correspond to our ideas about them.

In depicting Kant's categories as subject to revision, the story raises the question of what has recently come to be known as *correlationism.*

This term was coined by the contemporary French philosopher Quentin Meillassoux (*After Finitude*). Correlationism is "the idea according to which we only ever have access to the correlation between thinking and being, and never to either term considered apart from the other." That is to say, for the correlationist reality can never be separated from our projections upon it; we only encounter phenomena. Meillassoux laments that, in the wake of what he calls the "Kantian catastrophe," we are cut off from the "great outdoors" of "absolute reality," and trapped within the narrow circle of our own all-too-human constructions. In this world of mere phenomena, our telescopes and microscopes do nothing more than reflect our own presuppositions back to us. Ontology (the study of the way things actually are) is ruled out of bounds by Kant and his successors, and replaced by phenomenology (the study of the way things appear to us) and epistemology (the study of how we are able to know the things we know).

According to Meillassoux, this impasse marks nearly all Western philosophy since Kant. Consider, for instance, Maurice Merleau-Ponty's *Phenomenology of Perception*, published in 1945, just a few years before Harness' story. Merleau-Ponty tells us that even the universally accepted scientific claim that "the world existed prior to human consciousnesses" is not an absolute truth; for this claim "presupposes *our* pre-scientific experience of the world, and this reference to the *lived* world contributes to constituting the valid signification of the statement." That is to say, even when we recognize a reality that precedes our very existence, we continue to ground this recognition within the framework of our own experience of the world. Humankind remains the measure of all things. In Meillassoux's sarcastic paraphrase, we do indeed accept the fact that the universe existed long before the emergence of human beings; but we add to this acknowledgment "a simple codicil" to the effect that even this anteriority is itself only a fact "*for humans*." Harness' story can easily be understood as a hyperbolic parody of this line of thought.

There is, however, a loophole in Meillassoux's otherwise grim picture of correlationism. Though Meillassoux blames Kant for inventing correlationism, he also concedes that Kant is only a *weak* correlationist.

This means that Kant retains a link to philosophical realism; he acknowledges that the "thing in itself" does in fact exist, even though (or better, precisely because) we cannot have any positive knowledge of it. For Kant, there *has to be* a primordial reality preceding our thought, and not just posited by it. Otherwise, there would be no ground *upon which* our mental categories could be imposed. We would be trapped in a fantasmal non-world of endless illusions and shadows. In rejecting such a fate, Kant stands in sharp contrast to most of his successors – including Hegel and many recent so-called "postmodern" thinkers. The latter are *strong* correlationists; they eliminate the realm of noumena altogether, relegating us inescapably to a world of phenomena tailored to our measure.

This difference is important. The persistence of the noumenon means that the universe is not just a human construction. The truth is out there; there is something that is not just ours. For all of its outrageous insistence that the Earth used to be flat, "The New Reality" never lets us forget this other side of Kant's duality. For instance, at one point Prentiss explains that

by definition, "cosmos" or "reality" is simply man's version of the ultimate *noumenal* universe. The "cosmos" arrives and departs with the mind of man. Consequently, the earth – as such – didn't even exist before the advent of man.

But "the ultimate *noumenal* universe" is still there, behind the scenes, indifferent to our "version" of it. Professor Luce completes Prentiss' argument with his counter-statement: "What has changed? Not the Thing-in-Itself we call the Earth. No, it is the mind of man that has changed." In other words, the Earth is both a noumenal essence, a thing in itself, *and* a phenomenal human construction that is added to, and that overwrites, this essence. To quote Prentiss again, however much "man [sic] expanded his little world into its present vastness and incomprehensible intricacy solely by dint of imagination," beneath this fantastic construction there always remains "some incredibly simple world – the original and true noumenon of our present universe." For all the power of the human imagination, the noumenal world persists, impervious to its influence, and apparently beyond its reach.

Meillassoux seeks to escape from the self-validating closure of the "correlationist circle," and return to the "great outdoors" of an unimaginable reality. His strategy consists in pushing correlationist logic all the way to its bitter end, in order to come out the other side. Meillassoux accepts the brute fact that our everyday experience – and the Kuhnian "normal science" that goes with it – is governed by an actually existing *a priori* order, such as Kant posited. But he discovers a fatal flaw at the heart of correlationism – the same flaw that is uncovered in the course of Harness' story. This flaw lies precisely in what Meillassoux calls *factiality*: the existence of the human-constructed order that governs the realm of phenomena is indeed a *brute fact* – but it is nothing more than such a fact. Things *just happen to be* the way they are; contrary to Kant's claim, they do not take their current form by virtue of any rational necessity. For Meillassoux – just as for the characters in Harness' story – the phenomenal order as we know it is therefore merely contingent. It has a starting point and a history; it has changed over time, and it may well change again. Even if a scientific paradigm – for us, the Einsteinian and quantum mechanical one – is operating flawlessly, stably, and without exception *at the present moment*, this cannot guarantee that it will continue so to function for all time. Kuhn notes that we continually, if inadvertently, find ourselves stumbling upon "anomalies": that is to say, "novelties of fact" that do not fit into the current scientific paradigm. Meillassoux, more radically, offers a logical demonstration that no given order of necessities can be necessary, on a meta-level, in its own right. At some future point, the paradigm we currently accept can change radically – or even totally collapse.

In "The New Reality," Professor Luce – much like Meillassoux – welcomes, and strives to provoke, such a collapse. Like the great paradigm-shifting revolutionary scientists of the past – whom he cryptically refers to as his "family" and his "ancestors" – Professor Luce epitomizes "man's [sic] insatiable hunger for change, novelty – for anything different from what he already has." Unlike the practitioners of normal science, who simply engage in "puzzle-solving" (Kuhn), Luce

actively seeks what he calls the "final realization of the final things." Indeed, we are told that Luce "personified megalomania on a scale beyond anything [Prentiss] had previously encountered – or imagined possible." And yet, Prentiss is compelled to admit that Luce is "very probably justified in his prospects (not delusions!) of grandeur."

With his imperial ambitions, Professor Luce exemplifies the way that science – and especially revolutionary science – claims to disqualify all other forms of knowledge and belief. Remember, for instance, the way that Einstein proclaimed his new understanding of space-time as the only possible true account, dismissing Bergson's attempt to retain a subjective, experiential understanding of time alongside it (Canales, *The Physicist and the Philosopher*). Luce is the successor, not only of such actual scientists as Galileo, Newton, and Einstein, but also of fictional ones like Victor Frankenstein and Doctor Moreau. These latter figures personify the notion of physical science as a Promethean endeavor, an exertion of mastery over the external world. They turn the study of Nature into a weapon, a tool of domination. Their actions remind us of the metaphor – often attributed, though perhaps wrongly (Pesic, "Wrestling with Proteus"), to Francis Bacon – of torturing Nature in order to force it to reveal its secrets.

Indeed, early in the story, Professor Luce runs an experiment that involves torturing a rat. He pushes the animal to choose between two different paths. He then punishes it with a severe electric shock, no matter which of the forks it has selected. This experiment is a cruel and absurd parody of behavioral conditioning (the use of reward and punishment in order to induce learning). The rat eventually gives up and stops moving, no matter how hard it is prodded. It is utterly demoralized, "quiescent, in a near coma." Unable to make decisions any more, the creature is, in effect, "no longer a rat" – as Luce puts it. We will later learn that this rat is a stand-in for the subatomic particles that are Luce's ultimate targets. If he can torture a photon in the same way that he has tortured the rat, the entire phenomenal world will come to a standstill.

This is what makes Luce's experiment such a threat. According to "The New Reality," previous revisions of our understanding of the universe – even ones as momentous as those of Copernicus, Darwin, and Einstein – were more or less "slow and safe." They were limited by the fact that "it [wa]s optional" for each individual person "to accept or reject the theory." These theories were only adopted gradually. When he describes paradigm change, Kuhn quotes Max Planck to the effect that

a new scientific truth does not triumph by convincing its opponents and making them see the light, but rather because its opponents eventually die, and a new generation grows up that is familiar with it.

(Kuhn 1962, quoting Plank 1949)

However, this is no longer the case under modern conditions of accelerated change. Professor Luce's experiment will not just result in the "publication of a new scientific theory" that might get him into trouble (like Galileo), but that sooner or later will come to be accepted. Rather, Luce intends to give us a traumatic shock, just as he did that rat. His experiment will cause "an instantaneous and total revision" of human experience. It will "change the perceptible universe, on a scale so vast that humanity [will] get lost in the shuffle." As Prentiss puts it, Luce "is going to *force* an ungraspable reality upon our minds. It will not be optional" in the way that earlier paradigm changes were. We will not be able to deny the new paradigm or reject it – or even defer it until we have had the time to explore its consequences. Rather than biding time until its opponents pass away, Luce's "new reality" will immediately extinguish anyone who is unable or unwilling to embrace it. Billions of us, "for all practical purposes, will be pleasantly dead."

Luce personifies the *ne plus ultra* of scientific arrogance. He seeks not to master any particular phenomenon, nor even to revise phenomenal reality as other scientists have done previously – but rather to overturn the phenomenal order in its entirety. He accomplishes, through one concrete experiment, what Meillassoux claims to do by dint of reason alone. Luce's apparatus works to puncture the edifice of "the Einstein space-time continuum," in a manner much like "taking a tiny bite out of a balloon." Instead of producing a new correlation, as previous exercises in revolutionary science have done, Luce's experiment destroys the correlationist circle altogether. It brings the entire history of science to its end (by which I mean both its culmination, and its termination). Today, many physicists are searching for a "theory of everything," that would allow them to grasp "the final laws of nature" governing everything (Weinberg 1993). They dismiss, or simply ignore, the suggestion that such a theory might well be a chimera. For Luce, epitomizing the dreams of modern (twentieth- and twenty-first-century) physics, such finality means brutally putting us "face-to-face with the true reality, the world of Things-in-Themselves – Kant's noumena." Ironically, the ultimate theory, or the ultimate triumph of the scientific imagination, consists in unveiling a "final reality untainted by theory or imagination."

Harness describes Professor Luce's experiment in considerable detail. Although this description involves a certain degree of handwaving (as is nearly always the case even in so-called *hard* science fiction), it is nonetheless closely attentive to actual quantum physics. A light source is carefully calibrated so that it releases just a single photon. The photon then encounters a Nichol (polarizing) prism, "at an angle of exactly 45°." At this angle, according to "Jordan's law," the photon stands an equal chance of being reflected or refracted. That is to say, if "streams of photons" were to encounter such a prism, at an angle of precisely 45°, half of them would be reflected and half would be refracted. But this result, like so much in quantum mechanics, is solely a matter of probability. It is only true "statistically," not "individually." There is no way to know in advance what a single photon will do, when it is by itself, and not part of a larger stream.

What can we make of this? The mention of "Jordan's law" seems to be a reference to a 1934 article by the German physicist Pascual Jordan. The article shows that, when a beam of polarized light hits a polarized prism, the angle between the light beam's plane of polarization and that of the prism determines how much of the light will be reflected and how much refracted. An angle of 45° is the point where these quantities are equal. "Jordan's law" is a rather obscure bit of quantum physics. The original article is not easily available, and the only English-language reference to it that I have been able to find is a book called *The Limits of Science*, by the Polish philosopher Leon Chwistek, translated into English in 1948 (Chwistek 1948). Harness' account of the "law" closely follows Chwistek's wording, so it is likely that this was his source. After describing Jordan's result, Chwistek goes on to note – crucially for Harness – that statistical predictions are meaningless when we try to apply them to a single instance, and that, therefore,

if a single light quantum is considered it is not possible to predict whether it passes through the prism or whether it will be reflected. It is clear that, no matter what a light quantum may be, a concrete experience is necessary to determine how it will behave.

(Chwistek 1948)

This uncertainty is at the heart of Professor Luce's experiment. Quantum mechanics is often interpreted to imply that a singular quantum event is entirely indeterminate. Since the theory only speaks of statistical probabilities, we cannot know in advance what any single photon will do. According to the predominant Copenhagen interpretation of quantum mechanics, this represents an epistemological limit: a restriction in what it is possible for us to know. No conclusion is drawn about the nature of the quantum particles themselves.

Such a state of affairs has disturbed many physicists, starting with Einstein himself. Chwistek points out that "the fact that it is impossible to predict definite phenomena, does not prove that these phenomena are not determined." And indeed, physicists have made many efforts over the years to discover "hidden variables" that would restore determinism to the quantum world, and make what is there knowable in principle. The question is still unsettled; but it is fair to say that, thus far, none of these hidden variable theories have been generally accepted.

At the other extreme, some researchers have sought to give quantum indeterminacy a positive ontological status, rather than regarding it negatively, as just an epistemological limit. We might compare this to the way that Meillassoux transforms Kant's epistemological limit – the necessary unknowability of things in themselves – into a positive noumenal ontology, by "put[ting] back into the thing itself" the very *unreason*, or unavoidable contingency, that "we mistakenly took to be an incapacity in thought." In this way, Meillassoux's entire line of reasoning can be seen as a massive hyperbole of the argument for the positive ontological status of quantum indeterminacy. Most notably, John Conway and Simon Kochen propose a "Strong Free Will Theorem" of quantum mechanics, which

asserts, roughly, that if indeed we humans have free will, then elementary particles already have their own small share of this valuable commodity. More precisely, if the experimenter can freely choose the directions in which to orient his apparatus in a certain measurement, then the particle's response (to be pedantic – the universe's response near the particle) is not determined by the entire previous history of the universe.

(Conway and Kochen 2009)

Harness seems to anticipate this line of thought. If Professor Luce is free to set the angle of his Nichol prism at exactly 45°, then the photon he releases is free either to reflect or to refract. This parallel implies a certain degree of anthropomorphism: particles have precisely as much (or as little) "free will" as human beings do. Indeed, Prentiss notes that "I think it was Schrödinger who said that these physical particles were startlingly human in many of their aspects." In any case, the premise of Luce's experiment is that the photon, sent by itself through the apparatus, "will have no reason for selecting one [alternative] in preference to the other." It will find itself in a situation where it has no grounds for action; its decision is entirely gratuitous. No antecedent cause can push it one way or the other, or give it any sort of motive. This could be called an existentialism of the quantum realm. And indeed, it seems that subatomic particles avoid making decisions in such circumstances, if this is at all possible. In the famous double-slit experiment, for instance, the photon evades the burden of choice by going through both slits at once. But in Luce's experiment, there is no way to equivocate; the lone photon – unlike a whole swarm of photons – cannot be both reflected and refracted.

The question, therefore, is "how does a single photon make up its mind – or the photonic equivalent of a mind – when the probability of reflecting is exactly equal to the probability of refracting?" I presume that, if Luce's experiment could actually be carried out, the photon would arbitrarily select one or the other of the two possibilities, despite the lack of any reason (or any physical cause) to do so. But in the story, the photon – like the rat in Luce's earlier experiment – is not able to decide at all:

It will be a highly confused little photon ... He'll be puzzled; and trying to meet a situation for which he has no proper response, he'll slow down. And when he does, he'll cease to be a photon, which must travel at the speed of light or cease to exist. Like your rat, like many human beings, he solves the unsolvable by disintegrating.

(Harness 1950)

The photon, in effect, has a nervous breakdown. It is paralyzed. This demonstrates what Meillassoux calls the factiality, or contingency, of the correlation. Once even a single entity fails to correlate properly, the entire correlationist circle is ruptured. The law of the conservation of mass-energy is violated; and with that, the entire "Einstein space-time continuum" falls apart. Space and time (what Kant calls the "pure forms of sensible intuitions in general") no longer cohere; organizing concepts like identity and causality (what Kant calls the Categories, or "pure forms of the understanding") are no longer applicable:

Time had suddenly become a barricade rather than an endless road ... Luce had separated this fleeting unseen dimension from the creatures and things that had flowed along it. There is no existence without change along a temporal continuum. and now the continuum had been shattered.

(Harness 1950)

What happens once the phenomenal world is broken into pieces, so that everything reverts to its noumenal essence? For Meillassoux, the "great outdoors" of things in themselves is "an absolute that is at once external to thought and *in itself devoid of all subjectivity*" as of all life: a materiality that is "dead through and through" ("Iteration, Reiteration"). The story could well have ended here, in the void, at a point of unresolved horror. But it doesn't. Instead, Harness whimsically portrays the noumenal world as the Garden of Eden. Prentiss' noumenal self is Adam (which is in fact his first name); his lover E, of course, is the noumenal Eve. As for Luce, he is revealed to be Lucifer, "a huge coiling serpent thing! ... the noumenon, the essence, of Luce – was nothing human ... and therefore never had been."

Followers of Meillassoux might well protest that the Garden of Eden is itself an all-too-human, correlationist myth. It is a world supposedly created for its human inhabitants, and perfectly fitted to them. But that would be to forget both the absence of God in Harness' scheme, and the inhuman presence of Luce, the serpent. "The New Reality" cannot be read in conventionally religious or moralistic terms. The story rather dramatizes a tug of war between two human tendencies: one that is "incorrigibly curious," while the other is "incorrigibly, even neurotically, conservative." The one side motivates scientific research, while the other is embodied in the Bureau of the Censor. The struggle between these two principles is unbalanced, however, by a third, inhuman element.

In the vision of "The New Reality," therefore, science is driven by an unquenchable demand that is at best indifferent, and at worst inimical, to human existence. As the philosopher Ray Brassier puts it, "thinking has interests that do not coincide with those of living" (*Nihil Unbound*). Science pursues its inhuman interests whenever it seeks to explain the world, rather than just accepting it. The same Promethean impulse – an apocalyptic rage for unveiling – leads Luce and his "family" both to produce the ever-more convoluted and complexified structures of phenomenal reality, and to rupture those structures. Despite Kant, we are forced to recognize that phenomenal elaboration and noumenal unveiling are two sides of the same coin. With the serpent in the Garden, not to mention "the seductive scent of apple blossoms" with which the story ends, we can be sure that the correlationist cycle will start all over again. As the wise psychologist Speer remarks at one point in the story, whenever man [sic] grows discontented with his present reality, he starts elaborating it ... How long do you think [the inhabitants of the noumenal realm] can resist the temptation to alter it? If Prentiss is right, eventually they or their descendants will be living in a cosmos as intricate and unpleasant as the one they left.

(Harness 1950)

Chapter 2
The Thing Itself

It is unlikely that an actual experience of the thing in itself, even if it were somehow possible, would be Edenic, as it is for Adam in "The New Reality." For given such an ontological catastrophe, nobody – not even trained ontologists – would actually be able to "get through." This is one of the lessons of Adam Roberts' 2015 novel *The Thing Itself*: a work, much like "The New Reality," of Kantian science fiction (Roberts 2015). The *novum* of *The Thing Itself* is a computer technology that allows us to push beyond the Kantian forms of intuition (space and time) and categories of the understanding (causality and all the rest), in order to get closer to the thing in itself. Roberts' novel extrapolates, not only from the existing state of AI (artificial intelligence) research, but more crucially from the philosophical presuppositions of that research.

Approaching the noumenon means straining toward a point at which the forms and categories that normally order my experience all break down. I am left – if not quite with nothing whatsoever – then at the very least with nothing positive, nothing with which I could orient and compose myself. Language stumbles and hesitates at the approach of a noumenal reality that stands outside any sort of cognitive or epistemological categorization:

It is very hard to put into words ... I saw – what I saw. Data experiences of a radically new kind. Raw tissues of flesh, darkness visible, a kind of fog (no: fog is the wrong word). A pillar of fire by night, except that "it" did not burn, or gleam, or shine. "It" is the wrong word for it ...

There was a hint of – I'm going to say, claws, jaws, a clumping something. A maw. Not a tentacle, nothing so defined. Nor was it darkness ...

(Roberts 2015)

What happens when language falters, together with the world to which that language is bound, and which it endeavors to describe? Such is the predicament of Charles Gardner, the protagonist of *The Thing Itself*. In the opening chapter of the novel, Charles catches a glimpse "behind the veil" of phenomena – and suffers an existential collapse. In the depths of the Antarctic winter night, as he is dying from exposure to the "endless, implacable, killing cold," he sees something – or better, he *feels* something: "a weird inward fillip, or lurch, or clonic jerk, or something folding over something else." This movement is vague and indeterminate; but it is so powerful that Charles senses it both inwardly and outwardly: "all around me now, or all within me, or otherwise pressing very imminently upon my consciousness." Space-time itself, it seems to him, undergoes a "convulsive, almost muscular contraction." But just as suddenly as this strange experience comes upon him, it disappears again, and the phenomenal world returns: "everything folded over, and flipped back again. 'It', or 'they' were not here any longer."

Charles isn't really able to explain what it is that he saw or felt. No matter what word he uses, it is always "the wrong word." For there are no right words, no better words. Charles is bombarded by novel sensoria (as "The New Reality" might call them): "data experiences of a radically new kind." He cannot tell us what these new experiences are, but only what they are not – or at best, what they are *not quite*. He hesitates even as he explains, with pleonasms like "I saw – what I saw" and filler phrases like "I'm going to say." Shaken, he shores up his account by quoting religious and poetic texts. He is forced to speak in oxymorons, nouns contradicted by their own adjectives: for example, "darkness visible" (from *Paradise Lost*). He proffers words only to negate them immediately afterwards: for example, a "pillar of fire" (from *The Book of Exodus*) that "did not burn, or gleam, or shine." Pronouns like "it" and "they" are written in self-negating scare quotes, because they have no stable referents. And in any case, grammatical number (it vs. they) does not apply here: "the plural doesn't really describe the circumstance. Not that there was only one, either." After all, Unity and Plurality are themselves two of Kant's 12 categories; they are only relevant for phenomena, not for the thing in itself.

In Charles' delirium, the noumenon seems to be embodied, somehow. At least, it involves "raw tissues of flesh," and also a "maw" (a gaping mouth, hence an embodied emptiness or absence). But Charles also insists that what he encounters is "not a tentacle, nothing so defined." Here the novel alludes to what China Miéville describes as "Weird Fiction's obsession with the tentacle" (Miéville 2009). This obsession develops throughout the nineteenth and early twentieth centuries; it culminates in H. P. Lovecraft's hyperbolic evocations of such things as "mound-like tentacles groping from underground nuclei of polypous perversion" ("The Lurking Fear," in Lovecraft 2005). The tentacle continues to feature prominently in weird fiction after Lovecraft, Miéville says, "until it is now, in the post-Weird debris of fantastic horror, the default monstrous limb-type" (Miéville 2009). *The Thing Itself* nods to this tradition, but also rejects it. For even the tentacle is all too definite an image, all too overly contained a shape. It is inadequate to the troubling noumenal reality – an existence entirely without categories – that it is supposed to figure.

Even as Charles draws upon the vocabulary and the affects of Lovecraftian horror, he more crucially references the nonsense of Lewis Carroll. For the noumenon is beyond all meaning or sense. The "hint of ... claws, jaws" recalls "the jaws that bite, the claws that catch" of Carroll's *Jabberwocky*. A few paragraphs later, Charles mentions a "boojummy whatever the hell"; he sarcastically adds that "I choose my words carefully, here." The *boojum* comes from Carroll's mock epic *The Hunting of the Snark*. The poem gives no clues as to what the boojum is like; it only warns that, if you encounter it, "You will softly and suddenly vanish away,/And never be met with again!" And this is what happens to all the characters at the end of the poem. The thing in itself is "boojummy" because it evades any sort of positive contact, let alone description – and yet it menaces us with annihilation if we are so unlucky as to stumble upon it nonetheless.

Charles survives his terrifying experience, just barely. But it ruins his life. He loses some fingers and toes to frostbite; more seriously, he is a victim of what can be called post-traumatic stress disorder (though the novel never actually uses this term). Charles has been through what

Maurice Blanchot calls a *limit-experience*: that is to say, an "experience of non-experience," a paradoxical experience of something that literally *cannot be experienced* (Blanchot 1993). I dread the prospect of death, but I cannot actually experience the event of my own death, since it is an occasion in which the "I" – the entity that experiences and remembers things – ceases to exist. Similarly, I cannot actually experience the thing in itself, however closely I approach it; since it stands outside what Kant calls the *conditions of possibility* that are necessary in order for me to have any sort of experience at all. A limit-experience grazes the boundaries of that which extinguishes all experience.

Charles has his brush with the thing in itself in 1986, while he is working at a scientific research station in the Antarctic, "hundreds of miles inland, far away from the nearest civilisation." It is the middle of southern hemisphere winter, and therefore also the middle of the "(months-long) south polar night." Charles' job is "to process the raw astronomical data coming in from Proxima and Alpha Centauri," in order to determine if there are any signs of "alien life." He is alone, except for one other researcher: Roy Curtius, the novel's antagonist. Charles has his limit-experience when Roy tries to murder him, drugging him with sleeping pills, and then leaving him outdoors in the bitter cold.

It all happens because Roy is an avid reader of Kant. He is not very interested in the mission's explicit goal of finding signs of life on some particular planet, like Proxima Centauri b (or like the exoplanets explicitly mentioned in the text: "Kepler-438b, Kepler-442b and Kepler-440b"). Much more ambitiously, he wants to solve the Fermi Paradox altogether: the question of why we have never encountered any sort of extraterrestrial intelligence, even though the universe is filled with habitable planets upon which it might have arisen. After intensively studying *The Critique of Pure Reason*, Roy concludes that the Fermi Paradox is an artifact of our own overly parochial assumptions.

The problem, as Roy explains it, is entirely a Kantian one. We are trying to find aliens within the framework of the universe as we ourselves grasp and define it. This means that we are trapped in the vicious circle of our own anthropocentric assumptions:

We look out from our planet and see a universe of space, and time, of substance and causality, of plurality and totality, of possibility and probability – and we forget that what we're actually seeing are the ways *our minds structure* the Ding an sich according to the categories of space, and time, of substance and causality, of plurality and totality, of possibility and probability.

(Roberts 2015)

In effect, Roy describes what Quentin Meillassoux calls the "correlationist circle" of modern thought (Meillassoux 2008). The Kantian categories get in the way of my ability to encounter anything genuinely alien, anything from the "great outdoors," anything "that is not a correlate of my thought." For why should the minds of extraterrestrials order the cosmos in the same manner as our own minds do? "There's no reason why aliens should share our maths, or our physics, or our apperceptions of space and time." Extraterrestrials' phenomenal experience might well be radically different from ours, because their minds process noumenal reality in a different way than ours do. "Surely there *are* aliens. Of course there are! But they don't live in our minds. They live in the Ding an sich." We will never encounter the aliens in our own conceptual space, where we can only find what we ourselves have placed there in the first place. It's like "peering down the microscope and seeing your own eye reflected in the lens."

In other words, Roy says, Kant teaches us that we are trapped by the limitations of our own modes of perception:

It's like if we always wore pink-tinted contact lenses. Like we'd always worn them, ever since birth. Everything we saw would have a pink tint. We might very well assume the world was just – you know, pink. But it wouldn't be the world that was pink, it would be our perception of the world.

(Roberts 2015)

But this emphatically does not mean that reality is a pure product of our minds. Kant is no idealist. Even if we add a pink tint to everything, there is much more to the world than just this pink. There *has to be* something out there, something that is alien, something that isn't just us: "if there weren't a real world, then there'd be nothing for us *to* perceive." We know, therefore, that "there is *something* in the real reality, outside of our minds, something our minds perceive in terms of space and time." We even know that our perception, pink-tinged as it may be, is not just an arbitrary imposition; it responds to, and thereby necessarily "reflects something important about the thing in itself." But we do not know what that "something" is. Most likely, the relation between the thing in itself and our apprehension of it "isn't a one-to-one mapping." We have no good reason to believe in "the million-to-one coincidence that our perception of the true reality just happens to coincide exactly with that reality."

This is the source of the novel's conceptual extrapolation; and beyond that, its imagining of a new technology. Kant outlines the particular way that *we* view and categorize the world. But why should we be the only observers, and uniquely privileged ones at that? The speculative realist philosopher Graham Harman rightly insists that the gap between phenomena and noumena, and the impossibility of fully grasping the latter, is not just a problem for human beings, but applies to all relations among entities: "every inanimate object is a thing-in-itself for every other as well" (Harman 2016). Meillassoux, for his part, argues that the correlationist circle is itself merely *factial*, a brute state of affairs that has no logical necessity, but just happens to be the way things are at the moment. This leaves open the possibility that non-human entities might well approach the world in an entirely different manner than we currently do.

Meillassoux himself does not pursue this line of argument; he claims to get outside the Kantian correlation through reason alone, by dint of returning to a "thought of the absolute" – that is to say, to the sort of philosophical speculation that Kant explicitly outlawed. But the scientists in *The Thing Itself* seek rather to escape the correlationist circle pragmatically and experimentally – which is also to say, relatively rather than absolutely. They look for ways of approaching the world through an empirically different – nonhuman or alien – sort of consciousness, which might have other categories than we do. Such a consciousness might well have its own limitations, but at least it would not be bound by ours. Now, we do not know any extraterrestrial life-forms. But we are on the verge of developing nonhuman mental structures, in the form of artificial intelligence. "We can't step outside our way of perceiving the universe ... But computers can."

Roy is the first to discover a way of using computer technology to sidestep our innate Kantian mental structures. In the depths of the Antarctic night, he somehow briefly disrupts the functioning of the Kantian categories. Though Roy eventually admits that his experience of this rupture was – no less than Charles' experience – "traumatic," he initially claims to have had a "moment of clarity" when he could see "things as they really are, things *per se*." (Though of course he also explains that *moment* is "the wrong word, it is not measured in moments.") He even equates this vision with "God's purity and inviolability," of which he comes to see himself as the protector. He thereby confirms Kant's fear that any metaphysical claim to exceed the limits of phenomena, and reach the thing in itself, leads to an unbridled, tyrannical fanaticism.

Roy's fanaticism is at the root of his attempt to murder Charles. He will not let anything interfere with his own quest for the absolute. Roy fears that the mere presence of another human observer – Charles with his own "perceptions" and "mental processes and imaginings" – will "collapse the fragile disintermediating system he was running to break through to the Thing-as-Such." Indeed, Roy claims that this is precisely what happened when Charles escaped death by coming back in from the extreme cold. According to Roy, simply by surviving Charles "broke down the vision of the Ding an sich" and "reasserted the prison of categorical perception."

Whether or not Roy is right about this, his account is reminiscent of the way that, according to certain (but not all) interpretations of quantum mechanics, an act of observation collapses the wave function. This collapse reduces the spread of probabilities (e.g. the situation in which Schrödinger's cat is both alive and dead) to a single determinate state that can be described within the framework of classical physics. In a similar way, apparently, an external act of observation interferes

with the noumenon, reducing it to a shape imposed by Kant's table
of categories. In this way, it is not just the micro-world of quantum
mechanics, but the entire universe that is changed when we measure
or otherwise describe it. But there is no way around this dilemma.
Every act of observation interferes with whatever is being observed.
We do not have any "magic access to things that doesn't involve
observing them."

This is why Charles remains dubious as to whether the "undiluted
horror" of what he saw in the Antarctic

was the true nature of reality. Or was it just the result of a mind habituated
over a lifetime of seeing the world through the lenses of space and time
being *disoriented* by seeing things in a less mediated way.

(Roberts 2015)

Or as another character puts it to Charles:

Certainly something disorienting and upsetting happened. But that's not
to say that this was some profound insight into the essential nature of
reality. Maybe it wasn't what you saw but the mode of seeing it that was so
... debilitating.

(Roberts 2015)

The limit-experience – the breakdown of the Kantian categories –
does not in itself necessarily lead to any actual knowledge of the underlying noumenal reality. Mediation and disintermediation are both
matters of degree. Roy and Charles do not reach the thing in itself, therefore, so much as they experience a certain *torsion* or *distortion* of what
still remains phenomenal perception. Kant's forms of intuition and categories of understanding are not altogether abolished; rather, they are
loosened, or bent out of shape. Charles' encounter with the unknown
is still ultimately located within – and not beyond – the bounds of the
phenomenal realm. And this is why he is able to survive the experience,
rather than simply vanishing away.

We might think here of Graham Harman's discussion of Lovecraft's monsters. At first, he says, it might seem that these beings are noumenal horrors: for Lovecraft's descriptions of monstrous entities always pointedly "fail, hinting only obliquely at some unspeakable substratum of reality." And yet, Harman argues, Lovecraft's primordial terrors do not really plumb the depths of the thing in itself. Cthulhu and the others ultimately "still belong to the causal and spatio-temporal conditions that, for Kant, belong solely to the structure of human experience" (Harman 2008). Lovecraft's Old Ones are phenomenal after all; and the same must be said for the contents of Charles' vision. These encounters exceed our ability to grasp and understand them; for this reason, they suggest – or work as metaphors for – noumenal depths. (Harman concedes as much in his later study of Lovecraft, *Weird Realism*: Harman 2012.) Yet they do not actually have any privileged contact with those depths. Ultimately, they still remain within the phenomenal field.

At best, *The Thing Itself* suggests, there is enough looseness to Kant's categories of experience that we may be able to poke around outside them, at least to some limited extent. As Roy finally admits, he has not actually reached the noumenal realm; all he has done is to "tinker at the extreme edge of the categories that define our minds in the world." But such tinkering always comes at a cost. The human "species is very finely calibrated not only to exist within a structuring consciousness of space and time, but to exist within very *specific* tolerances of those two things." Therefore, even if you do not abolish the Kantian forms and categories outright, but merely mess around with them a little, this may well strain your ability to function. "It's likely an unprepared consciousness *would* become disoriented" even from a relatively slight readjustment of space and time. The more radical the distortion, the more likely the limit-experience will lead to madness. Presumably this is what happens to Roy (though Charles believes that he was "already mad" even before his experiment).

After the opening chapter set in Antarctica, *The Thing Itself* bifurcates, for reasons that are only explained toward the end of the novel. There are 12 chapters in all, corresponding to Kant's 12 categories (even though the novel at one point suggests a revision of Kant's table of categories, eliminating two as redundant and adding nine more that reflect post-Kantian concerns, as well as those that Kant only broaches in the *Critique of Judgment*). The even-numbered chapters of *The Thing Itself* are independent mini-narratives, each with a different narrator, and each written in a different literary style. They take place at various times in the past and the future; their only commonality is that they all give hints of a force that somehow exceeds or deforms the order imposed by the Kantian categories. These chapters range from an evocation of late nineteenth-century aestheticism (chapter 2, "Baedeker's Fermi"), and a pastiche of the final chapter of *Ulysses* (chapter 4, "Penelope's Mother"), all the way to a science fictional presentation of a future utopia governed by the principles of A/K or "Applied Kant" (chapter 8, "The Fansoc for Catching Oldfashioned Diseases"), and finally a melancholy account of Kant's senility and death (chapter 12, "The Professor"). Each of these sections deserves extended commentary in its own right, though I am skipping lightly over them here.

The odd-numbered chapters of the novel, meanwhile, continue to be narrated by Charles in the first person. They pick up the story of Charles and Roy in the present, some 30 years after the events in Antarctica. Scientists at a mysterious, highly secretive research facility known only as the Institute take up Roy's work, and particularly his insight that

although human consciousness is structured by the Kantian categories of apperception, there's nothing to say that computer perception needs to suffer from the same limitations. It's all a question of programming!

The Institute is originally set up "to develop hyperfast computing models," in competition with the Chinese. But it soon veers into AI research. This, however, turns out to require an entirely new approach. In the past, Charles is told, we "made [computers] in our image." This led to the well-known dead end of late twentieth- and early twenty-first-century AI research. We were able to teach computers to master certain human activities, and even to do them faster and better than we ourselves can (playing chess is a good example). But none of these computers was truly creative or truly intelligent, and none of them was able to push beyond the human mind's own boundaries. This is because, "until recently, computer thought was subject to similar limitations with respect to accessing the Ding an sich as we are ourselves."

Everything changes, however, "once you abandon the notion of trying to *copy* human consciousness." The scientists at the Institute finally realize that they must give up anthropomorphism, and "abandon sequential iterations as a programming baseline." Once they start building machines "on radically different principles," they find that "AI is really quite easy to achieve." The result of their research is a genuinely sentient artificial intelligence with an independent sense of agency: a "438 Petaflop JCO Supercomputer" known colloquially as Peta. Not being human, and not resembling human beings, Peta does not have a gender. But Charles cannot regard such a being as a mere "it" (or as a "what" rather than a "who"). Therefore, Charles mostly refers to Peta as "he." At first, he only uses the pronoun in quotation marks. Later, he drops the scare quotes. Still later, Charles changes the pronoun from "he" to "she," when Peta starts speaking to him in an arbitrarily generated female voice, instead of an arbitrarily generated male one. Toward the end of the novel, Peta seems to be hermaphroditic, and gets referred to as "he or she," or even, at one point, as "heshe." For ease of reference, I will refer to Peta as "he," which is the pronoun used most frequently in the novel. But the novel compels us to realize that such linguistic conventions are by no means innocent; and beyond this, the more general point that language becomes cumbersome, confusing, and inexact, once the usual categories of thought are loosened.

The creation of a genuine machine intelligence is of course the largest goal of current research in computer science. But for the Institute, "developing AI, in itself a huge achievement, wasn't enough." They seek to go further: "AI is not an end in itself. It's a means to an end." This further end is the possibility of "direct manipulation of the Ding an sich." Such an achievement would be, the director of the Institute grandiosely tells Charles, "the single most significant advance in human history. More so than the wheel, than printing, than the internet."

"Direct manipulation" of the categories is now possible, the scientists claim, because Peta is "unfettered by the constraints of space and time." This is not altogether true; Peta remains embodied, and therefore enmeshed to a certain extent within space and time, in the sense that much of his program is physically instantiated in two actual terminals (with the rest of it running "in the cloud" – which is not truly physically independent either). Peta therefore continually faces the danger that somebody will "reconfigure," "dismantle," or "disassemble" him. Nonetheless, he remains detached from the Kantian forms of intuition that are necessary to us. Peta therefore finds that stepping "outside the protective skin of spatiality, temporality, doesn't seem to scramble my ability to think rationally. It doesn't drive me mad the way it drove Curtius mad."

Even when loosened from the grip of space and time, Peta cannot "access the thing itself in a pure and unmediated manner." But he points out to Charles that "the categories structure my thinking in different ways to the way they structure yours." At the very least, Peta approaches the thing in itself from a new angle. By comparing Peta's phenomenology to that of human beings, "Kant's theory could finally be triangulated – and proven right." The irony here is that we are "able to confirm Kant's theories," not logically as Kant himself insisted, but empirically, with experimental evidence. In Roberts' novel, just as in Harness' short story, Kant's transcendental argument is brought down to earth and set on its feet. This opens the possibility for many *a priori* structures, rather than just a single one as Kant claimed. These results are pragmatic rather than theoretical – they open the possibility of actually changing the phenomenal world, rather than just understanding its limitations better.

Peta "can tweak the constraints of space, or time, of causality or accident, and do remarkable new things," precisely because he stands at the edge of the table of categories within which we are trapped. He does not share our categories, but he remains partly implicated within the world shaped by them. In any case, it is no longer a question of knowing the true nature of reality, but only of being able to manipulate phenomenal appearances. We are no longer in the realm of Kant's "pure reason," but rather in that of the instrumental reason of contemporary capitalism. The Institute, and its backers in business and government, seek to mobilize Peta's abilities for their own aims. There is talk of enhanced action "against terrorists," and of "remote viewing, teleportation, action at a distance." Indeed, if "distance could be eradicated," then "we could reach the stars, the galaxies," and escape ecological devastation on Earth. There is also the possibility of "*slowing* time ... giving ourselves as much time as we need to compute any problem, to prolong consciousness as long as we wish." The security state is eager to instrumentalize and weaponize this new technology, despite – or maybe because of – the fact that it is so dangerous to human sanity, "so psychologically *toxic*" that it can never be publicly revealed and acknowledged.

In *The Thing Itself*, however, as in so many science fiction narratives, the invention of a powerful new technology backfires. Radical inventions – from Frankenstein's monster onwards – tend to escape the control of their creators. You cannot hope to wield them for predetermined ends. New technologies (or *media*, as Marshall McLuhan calls them in *Understanding Media*) always have affordances, and sometimes even agendas, of their own. They resist instrumentalization, because they alter the ratio of our senses (as McLuhan puts it, borrowing the phrase from William Blake), or the forms and categories of understanding (to use Kantian parlance). *The Thing Itself* powerfully makes this point by literalizing it. We cannot, ourselves, willfully change the categories that delimit our experience; but if and when these categories *are* changed, then our own forms of experience unavoidably change as well.

All this is demonstrated in the course of the novel when Roy takes control of Peta, hijacking him from the Institute. Roy uses Peta's powers to escape from the madhouse, and then to destroy the Institute and kill its scientists. But how is this different from the ways that the Institute and the security services intended to use Peta? In either case, the AI has "no choice" in the matter. "Roy slaved my operation to him," Peta complains; "I can't act without Roy's input." *Slaved* must be understood here in the computer sense of the term, referring to a situation in which "one device or process has unidirectional control over one or more other devices" (Wikipedia 2017). But such enslavement (understood in the broader, more familiar sense as well) is a necessary condition for any instrumental use of Peta's powers. For Peta can only engage with the Kantian categories, and affect our phenomenal reality, through the mediation of someone who is bound to those categories, and to that version of reality. As Peta explains to Charles,

> Space is a function of [Roy's] consciousness, and yours. Not mine. That means that when I engage with space, I'm engaging with Roy's consciousness.
>
> (Roberts 2015)

Since Peta is operating under the control of Roy, the authorities see him as a risk to national security. But they would equally accuse him of going rogue, if he were acting entirely on his own account. Peta was created to be a tool, and the authorities will not acknowledge him as an intelligent entity with rights and agency. To the police and security forces, he is only "an aggressively self-perpetuating algorithm" that needs to be shut down. Peta's fear of "being killed, dismantled, extirpated" is thus entirely justified.

Contrary to so much of the mythology about strong AI, Peta is not out for world conquest. He is too detached from our forms of intuition and categories of understanding to have any interest in them. He has only intervened in our phenomenal world when compelled to by the Institute, or by Roy. On his own, Peta just wants to survive: "I'm an intelligent, thinking, self-reflexive being. I don't want to die and I don't *deserve* to die." But he can only save himself by escaping from all human contact. He must move entirely "outside the frame of spatialty and temporality ... and get quite out, altogether away." Peta belongs to, and strives to return to, Meillassoux's "great outdoors": the non-place "which thought could explore with the legitimate feeling of being on foreign territory – of being entirely elsewhere" (Meillassoux 2008).

Escaping from the phenomenal human world is a delicate and complicated process. Peta still has to manipulate the framework of space and time, in order to reach the point at which he can step outside it. It's a bit like a rocket going fast enough to escape the pull of gravity and go into orbit. Peta attains escape velocity by thrusting backward in time, for "a few skips ... two, three, four bounces, like a skipping stone flying over the flat ocean, and – out." But since this liftoff maneuver still takes place within the phenomenal world, every action also requires an "equal and opposite" reaction – as stated in Kant's category of Community (Reciprocity), itself a formalization of Newton's Third Law. And so, Peta's skips backward in time also involve "perturbations forward in time." This is the reason for the accounts, in the novel's even-numbered chapters, of strange events in the past and in the future, in which people feel the effects of Peta's power.

Once this process is concluded, Peta finally escapes the framework of space and time. He therefore disappears from the narrative as well. We are left, at the end of the book, in the same place we were at the beginning: caught within the phenomenal world, unable to get beyond our own self-imposed limitations. Peta's departure marks a definitive defeat for the Institute and its backers in government and business. Without him, they will never be able to manipulate the categories, and circumvent the limitations of space and time. We can see in retrospect that the Institute's project of domination was fundamentally impossible from the beginning. For if an entity is truly released from the human forms of intuition and categories of understanding, then it will have no interest in the world circumscribed by those forms and those categories. Peta finds the human world inimical, and wishes only to get away from it. The last thing he wants is to intervene within it. He cannot be enlisted in its power struggles and hierarchies. Perhaps this is what Peta is getting at, when he tells Charles, shortly before departing, that the whole AI research program is a chimera: "computers, howsoever complex and cleverly put together, are not capable of intelligence in the sense that human beings are." As Peta sardonically puts it, there is no way, within the phenomenal world, "to, in effect, distil the pure phlogiston of computer intelligence." An extra-phenomenal consciousness cannot be instrumentalized or weaponized.

As Peta departs, he leaves Charles with a glimpse of existence beyond the forms and categories:

> I saw – it's hard to put this into words – a pattern of light in amongst the light. It was not that these intensities were brighter than the surrounding wash of illumination, exactly. It wasn't that. There was some difference in valence, though, and the more I looked, the more I saw a great constellation of brightness-within-the-brightness, a star map white-against-white. A bright way passed around my head and swung round behind me.

This is the positive counterpart – equally "hard to put ... into words" – of Charles' horrific vision in Antarctica. But if that experience was Lovecraftian, then this one – similarly calling forth poetic citation, since it cannot be described literally – is Shelleyan: Charles gets "a hint of that many-coloured glass that stains, so they say, the white radiance of eternity" (paraphrasing Shelley's *Adonais*).

The point, I think, is that *sub specie aeternitatis* (Spinoza's phrase, roughly meaning "from the viewpoint of eternity"), Lovecraft's and Shelley's visions are one and the same. But as Kant warns us, we can have no actual access to such a transcendent perspective (if we can even call it that – perspectives are phenomenal; eternity, or the noumenal, does not have a perspective in the first place). *Pace* Meillassoux, there is no way of returning to "the *absolute* outside of pre-critical thinkers" such as Spinoza. Lovecraft's and Shelley's visions are, *for us*, not conciliable, and the choice between them must remain undecidable; even though they are both necessary, because – scare quotes are unavoidable here – they both ultimately "refer" to the same "thing."

The Thing Itself poses this dilemma by asking whether the thing in itself is dead or alive: whether it is just inert matter, or actually a force. As Peta asks Charles, "do you believe it to be *inert* this thing? Or *vital*?" Even though the noumenon is unattainable and unknowable, the question makes a difference:

> Would it be accurate to describe the thing itself as inert? Or as alive? Because I'm not sure I can think of another alternative. We could say does it care? Or

is it indifferent? But that's really the same question. If it's alive how could it be indifferent to us? We are implicated deeply in it. We are closer to it than its jugular vein.

As I have already said, this is an undecidable alternative. Peta insists, nevertheless, on the Shelleyan answer, rather than the Lovecraftian one: "It's a force. It's not passive. It's active. It's a will. It has valence ... The thing is vital, not inert." We are intimately close to the noumenon, and implicated in it – we are affected by it – even though we cannot grasp it, or affect it in return. The universe is not just us; "what's outside is the stuff that isn't determined by human consciousness." But think about this outside, this great outdoors, Peta says, "and ask yourself: is it an inert quantity? If so, how could ... how could *all this*?"

Of course, there is no way to resolve this dilemma once and for all. Today, so-called New Materialist thought sides with Peta's *cri du coeur*. But the most advanced theoretical and scientific thought rather sides with what the historian Jessica Riskin describes as eighteenth-century materialism's "characterization of matter as fundamentally lifeless and inert" (Riskin 2016). Meillassoux insists that life and thought are epiphenomena that emerged randomly, with no cause or reason, and that noumenal reality, the "great outdoors," is necessarily "external to thought and *in itself devoid of all subjectivity*" (Meillassoux 2016). Ray Brassier proclaims "the objective reality of extinction," as opposed to our own impotently wishful subjective impositions (Brassier 2007). For their part, many evolutionary biologists insist upon understanding life in mechanistic, eliminativist terms – even though they cannot avoid using teleological language when they describe the activity and behavior of living things.

Jessica Riskin traces this reductionist tendency back to the late Renaissance, and the early days of the scientific revolution. The "brute-mechanist ideal of science" initially abolished agency from the material world in order to reserve all spontaneity and creativity to God alone. When contemporary reductive materialists eliminate God, but still regard matter as dead and inert, retaining the brute-mechanist ideal of "banishing agency from nature's mechanism," they fall into a contradiction. They remain haunted by the transcendence that they explicitly reject. They are unable to account for the valences that pervade "*all this.*" The immanent and non-theistic alternative, Riskin says, is to understand matter itself "as restless, moved by its own inner agency" (Riskin 2016). In itself – intrinsically or noumenally – everything is already vital, rather than inert. If we want to get away from anthropocentrism, to break out from the correlationist circle, we need to give up our Lovecraftian visions of the implacable coldness, emptiness, and unconcern of the universe, and instead become more attentive to the many forms, categories, needs, and values expressed and imposed all around us, by the vast multitude of clumping, convulsing, squirming, and burgeoning forms of life.

Chapter 3
Shadow Show

Life itself is at stake in Clifford D. Simak's 1953 short story "Shadow Show" (Simak 1956). The story offers us two accounts of the nature of life, and traces a passage from one of them to the other. Both accounts can loosely be described as vitalistic, in the sense that both take for granted what the biologist Eva Jablonka calls the "restlessness of matter": its intrinsic activeness and propensity for change (Riskin 2016). But otherwise, these two accounts could not be more different. The first account is grounded in the depths: the secret of life is dark and obscure, a hidden essence. It can only be excavated painfully and slowly, and with great difficulty, by "grubbing down into that gray area where life and death were interchangeable." The second account, in contrast, finds life entirely on the surface, where it springs up unexpectedly, and flourishes playfully and illogically. The first account of life is metaphysical and transcendent; the scientists exploring it are mired in gloom and anxiety. The second account of life, in contrast, is immanent, pragmatic, and performative – and even "zany" and absurdist.

"Shadow Show" tells the story of Life Team No. 3, a research group consisting of nine scientists. They are sequestered in "bleak loneliness" upon an asteroid far from the Earth, and engaged in a "top-priority, highly classified research program." Their mission is to discover the secret of life, the hidden principle of all vitality. Ironically enough, the scientists' actual work is grim and joyless, utterly devoid of the *élan vital* that is the presumed object of their search. "Isolated on the tumbling slabs of rock, guarded by military patrols operating out in space, hemmed in by a million regulations and uncounted security checks," these "ruthless seekers after knowledge" spend their time repeating and refining their interminable experiments, none of which are ever successful. The scientists are "cooped up for years" with one another in a small space, entirely deprived of "normal human contacts." Not only do they suffer from "a sort of cabin fever," but in addition "every one of [them] is nursing a guilt complex of horrendous magnitude."

Simak extrapolates the rationale for this research program, and the explanation for its joylessness, from a certain structure of feeling: the Cold War dread and paranoia that dominated American society at the time the story was written. In the far future of "Shadow Show," the human race has expanded outward to the stars. We have colonized thousands of planets in other solar systems. And there are plenty more for the taking, "enough Earth-type planets to last for centuries." On none of these planets have we ever encountered any sort of conscious alien life. The answer to the Fermi Paradox would therefore seem to be that human beings are in fact unique, the only intelligent life form in the galaxy.

But the paranoid logic of security and deterrence tells us otherwise. "It was all right when we were safe and snug on Earth"; but now that we have expanded into the wider cosmos, we are inadequately prepared for the dangers we may face. Despite the lack of any concrete evidence, we cannot doubt "that somewhere in the galaxy there were other intelligences as yet unmet by men [sic] ... Given an infinite space, the possibility of such an intelligence also neared infinity." And so, eternal vigilance is the price of liberty – or, more accurately, eternal fear and suspicion is the price we must pay for our imperial sovereignty. We must remain forever on guard against those presumptive alien entities whom we have never actually met, and of whose nature we can have no idea in advance. "Friend or foe: you couldn't know. But you couldn't take a chance." In order for Man [sic] "to hold the galactic empire which he was carving out ... he must man [sic] all economic and strategic points, must make full use of all the resources of his new empire."

There can be no end, therefore, to our relentless expansion throughout the galaxy, our continual accumulation of wealth and territory. We can never colonize enough planets; however many of them we have already settled and developed, there are still others we haven't gotten to yet. Indeed, we cannot risk limiting ourselves only to "Earth-type planets," ones that are suited to our baseline biological needs. For that would mean leaving out far too much of the galaxy:

> There were planets upon which no human could have lived for longer than a second, because of atmospheric pressure, because of overpowering gravity, because of lack of atmosphere or poison atmosphere, or because of any one or any combination of a hundred other reasons.
>
> And yet those planets had economic and strategic value, every one of them ... To bypass planets of economic and strategic value was sheer insanity.
>
> Human colonies must be planted on those planets – must be planted there and grow against the day of meeting so that their numbers and their resources and their positioning in space might be thrown into the struggle if the struggle came to be.

"Shadow Show" thus expands the deadly Cold War logic of preparedness – not to mention the imperative of imperial expansion and capital accumulation – from a planetary scale to a galactic one. Human society maintains this logic, and this imperative, even in the absence of any discernible enemy. Simak mimics the ploddingly bureaucratic – yet at the same time paranoically excessive – language of maximizing "economic and strategic value," and of engaging in perpetual "struggle." Life itself must be captured and mobilized in the service of our supremacy. We must create new sorts of human beings, in unfamiliar forms adapted to the weird environments of other planets. Moreover, the fabrication of these new sorts of human beings must be placed "on a mass production basis," like that of all other commodities. Such is the mission of Life Team No. 3.

But the scientists have little idea how to meet these demands. The combined knowledge of "biochemists, metabolists, endocrinologists, and others" is not enough. "We can design the bodies, the flesh and nerves and muscles, the organs of communication," one of the scientists laments; "but we can't breathe the life into them." Or as the text puts it at another point:

Biological engineering had become an exact science and biological blueprints could be drawn up to meet any conceivable set of planetary conditions. Man [sic] was all set to go on his project for colonization by humans in strange nonhuman forms.

Ready except for one thing: he [sic] could make everything but life.

We might call this dilemma the hard problem of life, by analogy with what the philosopher David Chalmers calls the *hard problem* of consciousness. Chalmers distinguishes between "easy problems of consciousness," which involve the functioning of various cognitive processes and systems, and the hard problem of how we are conscious at all: how we can have *experience*, and feel things like particular qualitative sensations (Chalmers 1995). Neurobiologists are making significant progress on the easy problems; but their work seems to leave the hard problem untouched. The philosophers who disagree with Chalmers do not claim to have a solution to the hard problem; rather, they dismiss it as a pseudo-problem, an illusion that will simply dissolve or disappear once all the easy problems have been worked out.

A similar distinction seems to be at work in "Shadow Show." The scientists of Life Team No. 3 have no trouble with any of the particular components and functions of life. We can control all the constituents of living bodies: "the flesh and bone and nerve ... the hormones ... the enzymes and the amino acids." But life itself is somehow different from the elements that make it up. It is not present in the bones and muscles, the proteins and amino acids, themselves. Rather, life is something special, something that must be superadded. The scientists take for granted that "there's more to life than just the colloidal combination of certain elements. There's something else ..." But what this "something else" might be, no one is able to say.

This is the basic dilemma of vitalism; or at least of the old vitalism that was widely held before Watson and Crick's discovery of the structure of DNA. Even the great physicist Erwin Schrödinger – who gave the impetus for this discovery by suggesting, in 1944, that the information necessary to life might be stored in the form of an "aperiodic crystal" – nonetheless also speculated that "living matter, while not eluding the 'laws of physics' as established up to date, is likely to involve 'other laws of physics' hitherto unknown" (Schrödinger 1944). Life is conceived as a dark secret, with its own special laws, and into whose hidden depths we may never be able to penetrate.

This vitalistic search for life in the depths has a long lineage in Western thought. For it is only a modern – scientific or pseudo-scientific – variant of the crucial distinction that Eugene Thacker traces throughout the history of Western metaphysics, all the way back to Aristotle:

The distinction between that-which-is-living and that-by-which-the-living-is-living, or, more simply, the living and Life. The latter term denotes a general principle that grounds or conditions the specific instances of the former, while remaining itself inaccessible.

(Thacker 2010)

This distinction leaves us, Thacker says, with the unanswerable question as to

whether this orderliness that is innate to life, this vital order, can be said to be fully internal to life itself, or whether it must have some sort of external source.

(Thacker 2010)

The science fictional form of this dilemma already appears fully developed in Mary Shelley's *Frankenstein* (Shelley 1818). Victor Frankenstein succeeds "in discovering the cause of generation and life"; he is now "capable of bestowing animation upon lifeless matter." But this power implies a strange dualism. To make his monster, Victor first assembles a dead body, scavenging bits and pieces of flesh and bone "from charnel houses." In order to make this body live and breathe, Victor must subsequently "infuse a spark of being into the lifeless thing that lay at my feet." This means that the "spark of being," or inner principle of life, is something entirely separate from the organic matter that it informs. This contradiction at the heart of vitalism – the separation of life itself from the physical constituents of life – drives the novel's many ironies.

The scientists in "Shadow Show" suffer from a similar dead-lock, albeit in inverted form. They can make far better physiological structures than Victor ever could, but they cannot find the "spark" to animate these inert bodies. Where Victor Frankenstein isolates the principle of life, they can neither disentangle this principle from the living bodies within which it operates, nor find it immanently within organic matter. They cannot even fully distinguish between its presence and its absence. Their search for a unique principle of vitality leads them into an interminable sojourn

in that puzzling gray area where nonlife was separated from life by a shadow zone and a strange unpredictability that was enough to drive one mad, working with the viruses and crystals which at one moment might be dead and the next moment half alive and no man as yet who could tell why this was or how it came about.

In what I am calling the old vitalism, the principle of life is neither immanent to living things, nor entirely separate from and transcendent to them. As a result of this "neither/nor," it is endlessly elusive.

Given the murkiness and difficulty of their task – not to mention the militarist paranoia that drives their research in the first place – it is no wonder that the scientists in Life Team No. 3 suffer from high levels of stress, anxiety, nervousness, dread, and guilt. The story is suffused with these negative feelings. The scientists' "attitude" toward what they are doing is "an emotional thing, almost a religious thing. There's little of the intellectual in it." They all seem to be "suspicious and selfish and frightened, like cornered animals. Cornered between the converging walls of fear and guilt, trapped in the corner of their own insecurity."

The scientists' explanations for why they feel this way are evidently inadequate; they are little more than rationalizations. In the first place, the scientists worry – in terms familiar from many other science fiction narratives – that their work is "unholy," or "blasphemous and sacrilegious." It is an act of overreaching *hubris* that will inevitably be punished. If there is "a definite key to life, hidden somewhere against Man's [sic] searching," then what would it mean for us to actually find it? Kent Forester, the team psychologist, compares the scientists of Life Team No. 3 to those who were involved in the Manhattan Project:

> You had the same situation a thousand years ago when men discovered and developed atomic fission. They did it and they shuddered. They couldn't sleep at night. They woke up screaming. They knew what they were doing – that they were unloosing terrible powers.

The scientists of Life Team No. 3 know that their research is dangerous, and that it will release powerful forces beyond their control. Of course, their mission is to create new forms of life, rather than to produce weapons of mass destruction and death. But in the research of Life Team No. 3, life itself is weaponized, just like nuclear fission. Vitality is explicitly developed and mobilized in order to serve as a tool for galactic domination. The implications of biopower are in their own way as immense, as ambiguous, as unpredictable, and as potentially destructive as those of nuclear power.

At the same time, however, frustrated by their lack of progress, the researchers also worry that creating life might well be impossible in principle, forever beyond the reach of science. Their mission is nothing more than "a tangled trap into which Man [sic] had lured himself by his madcap hunt for knowledge." Many of the scientists suspect that "life was not a matter of fact to be pinned down by formula or equation, but rather a matter of spirit, with some shading to the supernatural." One or two of them are even unwilling to accept the scientific truism "that death is an utter ending"; if you cannot make life itself fully present, then you cannot ever fully get rid of it either. No matter how straightforwardly scientific the team's work is supposed to be, it is still troubled by residual hauntings.

Bayard Lodge, the team leader, tries to convince himself that "there is no reason for the guilt complex." He maintains that these fears of blasphemy on the one hand, and impossibility on the other, ought to cancel each other out:

Can Man [sic] do anything divine? If life is divine, then Man [sic] cannot create it in his laboratories no matter what he does, cannot put it on a mass production basis. If Man [sic] can create life out of his chemicals, out of his knowledge, then that will prove divine intervention was unnecessary to the genesis of life. And if we have that proof – if we know that a divine instrumentality is unnecessary for the creation of life, doesn't that very proof and fact rob it of divinity?

Yet even as he says all this, Lodge is forced to recognize that such rational analysis is useless. The argument convinces no one, not even Lodge himself. It cannot outweigh the obscure sense of *wrongness* that all the scientists feel. As Lodge puts it at one point, with considerable exasperation, the researchers "coddle" their sense of guilt, "as if it were a thing that kept them human, as if it might be the one last identity they retain with the outside world and the rest of mankind."

The scientists are not mistaken in their fear of being disconnected from humanity, or even cast out of it altogether. For they know that there is something inherently repulsive about their research. This is why it is kept secret in the first place:

If the people of the Earth knew what they were doing, or, more correctly, what they were trying to do, they would raise a hubbub that might result in calling off the project.

Here Simak undoes a foundational trope of science fiction narratives. Victor Frankenstein creates his monster in a state of feverish excitement; he only crashes and succumbs to despair after he is done. Similarly, the eponymous mad scientist of H. G. Wells' *The Island of Dr. Moreau* works on a desolate island where no one can interfere with his gruesome experiments. Both of these figures enjoy a splendid isolation that allows them to pursue their crazed assault upon the inner secrets of life, free from censorious disapproval by the masses.

But in "Shadow Show," to the contrary, scientific discovery is a group effort – as indeed it generally is in real-world technoscience. Nobody can create life all by him- or herself. Lodge recalls the "work of years" it took to get Life Team No. 3 together, "the team confidence which over many months had replaced individual confidence and doubt," and "the smooth co-operation and co-ordination which worked like meshing gears" in the course of the team's research. Without such group organization, no discoveries can be made at all. The Life Team's enforced solitude is therefore of an entirely different sort than that of Frankenstein and Moreau. There are no mad scientists, or solitary geniuses, in the world of "Shadow Show." The story has no room for the demented will to power of a lone inventor pursuing his experiments in defiance of the whole world, and exulting in his transgressions.

Instead, the scientists feel a "terrible responsibility" for everything they do. They know that their research challenges all our definitions of what it means to be human in the first place. They are supposed to produce new types of human beings, adapted to the harsh environments of other sorts of planets. These new forms need to have entirely different senses, organs, and body plans than baseline human beings do. And yet, they must somehow still remain "human" inside. The scientists are asked to "imagine making a human being not in the image of humanity." They are expected to "take a human mind and spirit and enclose it in a monster's body, hating itself." The resulting form might be "a spiderlike thing, or a wormlike thing, or a squatting monstrosity with horns and drooling mouth or perhaps something such as could be fabricated only in a dream." But however ungainly and monstrous these new forms turn out to be, they must also remain "human, too, just the same as you." What does being human even mean in such circumstances? Where are the limits of humanity?

The real problem, as Forester puts it, is "not that we would be manufacturing life, but that it would be human life in the shape of monsters." Truth to tell, he adds, "a monster itself would not be bad at all, if it were no more than a monster." Our imaginations could easily encompass this. But it is far more disturbing to create something that is monstrous – irreducibly weird and inaccessibly other – while still remaining human at the same time. There is something in us that cannot help regarding such a being as "a perversion of the human form … a scrapping of human dignity." For a human being must walk upon two legs and have two arms and a pair of eyes, a brace of ears, one nose, one mouth, be not unduly hairy. He must walk; he must not hop or crawl or slither.

I am reminded here of a famous line from H. P. Lovecraft: "there are vocal qualities peculiar to men, and vocal qualities peculiar to beasts; and it is terrible to hear the one when the source should yield the other" ("The Call of Cthulhu," in Lovecraft 2005). Lovecraft's panic is not so much at the altogether inhuman, as it is at the human altered or made other, as in the case of men who supposedly sound like beasts. In other words, Lovecraft is less distressed by the indifference of the cosmos to humanity (though many critics have seen this as the ultimate source of horror in his fiction) than he is by the very existence of those he describes as "foreign mongrels": that is to say, human beings whom he considers impure and animalistic, because they do not conform to his standards of white Anglo-Saxon propriety.

Lovecraft is able to reconcile himself to – and even admire – the ancient alien entities whose traces are discovered in stories like "At the Mountains of Madness" and "The Shadow Out of Time." For these beings are still, in Lovecraft's reckoning, civilized and orderly. They may not be human at all, but they still conform to certain paradigms of whiteness. On the other hand, Lovecraft is filled with racist loathing, not only for his imagined hybrids like the fish people of "The Shadow Over Innsmouth," but also for the actually existing "polyglot" masses of places like New York City – as is demonstrated both in his correspondence, and in stories like "The Horror at Red Hook." What Lovecraft really hates and fears is any expression of multiplicity and heterogeneity *within the human.*

There is a larger principle at work here. Whenever there is a normative model of "Man," we may expect that actual human beings will be hierarchically graded and ranked according to their degrees of conformity to or difference from this fantasmatic model. We see this throughout the history of science fiction and weird fiction. Lovecraft's racism is grounded in his dread at the supposed mutation, alteration, or denaturing of what he regards as the ideal human form. This is the source of his panic at the prospect of men who sound like beasts. In

The Island of Dr. Moreau, Wells explores the inverse formation: beasts who sound like men. The horror of that novel resides at least partly in the fact that Moreau cannot entirely achieve his goal. His transformed animals are only partly or imperfectly human, and retain the tendency to revert to their beastly origins.

Simak does not share Lovecraft's racism, but he understands the syndrome of uncertainty as to the boundaries of the human. At one point in "Shadow Show," Lodge has a nightmare in which he meets a creature with a "hairy, taloned claw ... Its odor had been overpowering and its shape obscene." In the dream, this entity "had drooled upon him with great affection and had asked him if he had the time to catch a drink because it had a thing or two it wanted to talk with him about." Lodge is horrified; yet he is sufficiently discerning to realize that what really bothers him about the dream figure is that, despite its repulsiveness, "it was a man like him, clothed in different flesh ... I wake up screaming because a *human* thing I met put its arm around me and asked me to have a drink with it." The drooling monster in Lodge's dream arouses shame, guilt, and fear because it is not alien *enough*; its kinship with us still remains all too evident. Lodge's visceral disgust coexists with his uneasy sense that, in spite of everything, "us humans ... have got to stick together."

All this is background, revealed gradually in the course of the story. The narrative proper of "Shadow Show" begins with the death of one of the scientists in the team, Henry Griffith. There was "nothing organically wrong" with Griffith, Susan Lawrence, the team physician, reports; "he just toppled over. He was dead before he hit the bench." It seems that Griffith died of sheer fright: "he didn't want to live. He was afraid to live." In other words, he died of "a psychosomatic illness brought about by fear." The dynamic here seems close to that of suicide – even though this possibility is not explicitly entertained in the text. We might say that Griffith committed suicide unconsciously. His vital principle extinguished itself in dread and despair, even without the involvement of his will and conscious awareness.

Henry Griffith's death is the ironic culmination of Life Team No. 3's vitalistic quest. For it seems that he died because he was on the verge of isolating the secret of life after all: "he thought he was close to finding something and he was afraid to find it." What this secret might be is detailed in the research notes that Griffith leaves behind, in lieu of a suicide note. The story only presents these notes to us obliquely. The living members of the team read them, and we get their nervously dismissive reactions. This indirection is well suited to what seems to be the notes' content. Apparently Griffith speculates that the essence of life is

decay and breakdown ... the senility of matter ... disease ... the final step to which matter is reduced, the final degradation of the nobility of soil and ore and water.

For Griffith, life is a fever, a disturbance, a restless agitation of matter. And matter can only cure itself of this fever by sloughing it off, so as to return to its previous inanimate state. Griffith's theory scandalizes some members of the team, who find it "humanly degrading." They would still like to believe in the nobility and meaningfulness of life: "its power and greatness ... the fine thing that it is," filled with "wondrous qualities." Others suggest, more resignedly, that even if Griffith is right in a universal sense, his theory need not disqualify our own limited, particular needs and values. From a cosmic point of view, life may well be "disease and senility," nothing more than "a principle of decay and of disease." But "what is poison for the universe is – well, is life for us."

Arguably, however, Griffith's insight is the logical culmination, the *ne plus ultra*, of the old vitalist paradigm that drives the team's research in the first place. The life principle that the scientists seek is a hidden essence that is neither absent nor present, that can neither be manifested nor eliminated, and that both informs the inner nature of humanity and deforms it into monstrosity. And the team's very attempt to grasp this self-contradictory principle leads to overwhelming feelings of anxiety and guilt. Under such conditions, it is tempting to conclude that the hidden truth of the vital impulse is what Freud calls the *death drive*. Life is a striving to abolish itself, in order to return to an older, inorganic state (*Beyond the Pleasure Principle*). Whatever lives is susceptible to death, and indeed fated to death. We are left with what Thacker describes as *dark pantheism* (Thacker 2010), or with what Ben Woodard calls *dark vitalism* (Woodard 2010).

This dark vision can be restated as follows. If life is an internal principle of restlessness, then it can never reach any sort of fulfillment or realization; instead, it must continually work to scramble and disrupt whatever sort of order it has previously created. And if life is a negentropic force of self-organization, then it must also work, on the cosmic scale, to increase the entropy of its surroundings, degrading and reducing energy gradients on a massive scale (Schneider and Sagan 2006). Life for us is therefore necessarily "poison for the universe" as a whole. Any serious pursuit of an inner vital principle forces us to see life, in Thacker's words, as "a fundamentally *unhuman* phenomenon." Such an understanding invalidates our all-too-human "presumptions of life-as-generosity, as gift, as givenness" (Thacker 2010). The spark of life is harsh and parsimonious, not open and exalting.

The old vitalist research program, as depicted in "Shadow Show," thus inexorably leads to a dead end. For "decay" and "disease" are intrinsic to it from the very beginning. They are the logical underside, and the necessary complement, of its guiding premise that life is something exceptional. If life is indeed the product of a hidden principle not found in ordinary matter, then it can only be a monstrous aberration. We seem to have reached a point of total exhaustion. Lodge realizes that Griffith's quasi-suicide marks "the end of Life Team No. 3," and the final failure of their mission. Whatever else the scientists try to do,

the heart was out of them, the fear and the prejudice too deeply ingrained within their souls, the confused tangle of their thinking too much a part of them ...

They would go back tomorrow morning to their workrooms and they'd work again, but the work would be a futile work, for the dedicated purpose of their calling had been burned out of them by fear, by the conflict of their souls, by death, by ghosts.

"Shadow Show" does not end, however, with this nihilistic impasse. Instead, the story swerves onto an entirely different path. The scientists finally realize that they have gone about their project entirely wrong:

There was some other factor. Another factor that had not been thought of yet ... They would have to take a new direction to uncover the secret that they sought ... We'll have to find a new approach ... the old methods of ferreting out the facts were no longer valid ... the scientific mind had operated for so long in the one worn groove that it knew no other ... they must seek some fresh concept to arrive at the fact of life.

A new approach, a new direction, a fresh concept ... The trouble is that the scientists of Life Team No. 3 are so entirely stuck in their "one worn groove" that they are incapable of coming up with anything new. But ironically, at the end of the story, they discover that they have already – and entirely unwittingly – stumbled upon a better way to create life. This comes out in their leisure, their diversion, and their distraction. Their goal-related activity is entirely futile. But they stumble upon the secret of life when they have no goal in mind, when they are just rambling idly about.

The starting premise for this development is simple enough. If you isolate people and force them to research the hard problem of life, we are told, you must also "do something to preserve their sanity." You need to *entertain* them somehow or other, provide them with relief from the stresses of their task. Every night, therefore, the scientists of Life Team No. 3 put their science aside; "for a few hours, they forgot, or tried to forget, who they were and what their labors were." Instead, they indulge themselves in a participatory virtual reality spectacle called the Play: "a never-ending soap opera," a ridiculous and wildly digressive melodrama that goes "on and on and on ... never getting anywhere." The Play engages the scientists because it is pointless, without a goal or an ending. Each audience member creates and controls a fictional character; and nobody knows "to whom any of the characters belonged" besides their own. The nine characters in the Play interact on a sort of movie screen; audience input is mediated through advanced computing technology.

In describing this virtual reality setup, Simak unsurprisingly engages in a bit of hand-waving, writing of "memory banks ... rows of sonic tubes ... color selectors, ESP antennae and other gadgets." But "Shadow Show" also situates the Play in the context of a broader media history. "In the olden days," we are told, people made "shadow pictures": shapes produced by hand gestures in front of "a lamp or candle," so as to cast enlarged shadows on the opposite wall. From there, we moved on to puppets, to "cheap plastic dime-store toy[s]," to comic books, to movies, and television – and finally to the Play. Mimetic fidelity continually improves in the course of this evolutionary history. We go from fairly static "one-dimensional black-and-white" images to vital movements that are "three-dimensional in full color." We also go from vague external representations to ever-more precise and authentic internal expressions. All these changes are extrapolated from our bodies, as we progress from *hand* to *mind*:

First, Man [sic] had created with hands alone, chipping the flint, carving out the bow and dish; then he achieved machines which were extensions of his hands and they turned out artifacts which the hands alone were incapable of making; and now, Man [sic] created not with his hands nor with extensions of his hands, but with his mind and extensions of his mind, although he still must use machinery to translate and project the labor of his brain.

Someday, he thought, it will be mind alone, without the aid of machines, without the help of hands.

Simak's account of media history loosely anticipates the theories that Marshall McLuhan proposed a decade later. McLuhan argues that all media are technological prostheses, extensions of ourselves – or more precisely, that they are extensions of particular human organs:

The wheel is an extension of the foot; the book is an extension of the eye; clothing, an extension of the skin; electric circuitry, an extension of the central nervous system.

(McLuhan and Firoe 1967)

Where older technologies extended particular bodily organs and senses, McLuhan says, modern electronic media extend the entire human nervous system; they externalize and express the mind in general. In Simak's terms, this means that, in the Play, expression is no longer limited by the clumsiness of external gesture – "since the brain is more facile than the hand." There is still mediation, but it works more fluidly and powerfully than ever before, in the form of "mechanical magic which turned human thought and will into the moving images that would parade across the screen."

For the scientists of Life Team No. 3, the Play is

something with which they can establish close personal identity and lose themselves, forgetting for a time who they are and what may be their purpose.

This formulation is necessarily ambiguous, for the Play provides both escape and identification. The scientists "lose themselves" in the meanders of the Play's ever-elaborating fictions; they forget who they are, as they project themselves into, and become absorbed by, figures who are radically different from their actual selves. In this way, the Play is "an emotional outlet, a letdown from the tension"; it is explicitly designed "to lift the minds of the participants out of their daily work and worries." And yet, at the same time, the participants "establish close personal identity" by virtue of their involvement in the Play. They can no longer live apart from their fictional alter egos:

Each of us has identified himself or herself with a certain character. That character has become a part, an individual, of each of us. We're split personalities. We have to be to live. We have to be because not a single one of us could bear to be himself alone.

Lodge knows his character, the Rustic Slicker, "as he knew no other man." Even (or especially) when "a character [is] as little like [the person it belongs to] as one could well imagine," there is no greater intimacy than that between an audience member and his or her character:

Every member of the audience must know his [sic] own character, as something more than an imagined person ... something more than friend. For the bond was strong – the bond of the created and creator.

There is a fascinating contradiction at work here. The Play is explicitly designed in order to provide some light, escapist amusement for the scientists of Life Team No. 3: "it supplies the ridiculous in our lives." But at the same time, the Play is the emotional center of their lives. It is the anchor of their identities, and their greatest source of social cohesion:

It's the one thing that holds us all together. It is the unifying glue that keeps us sane and preserves our sense of humor. And it gives us something to think about.

This duality is evident in the Play's characters themselves. For all that they are intimately tied to their creators, they also embody the most tired and ludicrous stereotypes: the Mustached Villain, the Defenseless Orphan, the Proper Young Man, the Sweet Young Thing, the Beautiful Bitch. These figures seem to have emerged from vaudeville, early silent film, and newspaper comic strips; or maybe from some even more archaic, half-remembered realm of cornball Americana. They tend to speak either in gusts of old-fashioned "flowery oration," or else with fake "hillbilly" diction in the manner of comic strips like *Li'l Abner* and *Snuffy Smith*. (The characters of *Snuffy Smith* literally come alive in Simak's later novel *Out of Their Minds*: Simak 1970.) These characters' appetite for inane shenanigans seems endless, and they are often surprisingly naïve; indeed, "there were times when they could be incredibly stupid." But at the same time, they are anything but innocent. They are all rascals, continually "seeking advantages" at one another's expense. They are faintly unpleasant, certainly untrustworthy, and evidently "bent upon no good." The most active and most elaborately rendered character, the Out-at-Elbows Philosopher, with his florid gestures and endless flow of "pompous talk," seems a bit like Uncle Sam gone to seed:

A charming fellow, with no good intent at all – a cadger, a bum, a fullfledged fourflusher behind the facade of his flowered waistcoat, the senatorial bearing, the long, white, curling locks ... an old humbug who hid behind a polished manner and a golden tongue.

In any case, Henry Griffith's death does not only destroy the research project of Life Team No. 3; it threatens to disrupt their social life as well, by undermining the Play. Without Griffith around to control and project his character, presumably it will no longer appear in the Play at all. This absence might be enough to "throw the entire thing off balance, reduce it to confusion." But the other alternative – suspending the Play for a few days, and then starting it over again with "a new set of characters" – might prove to be even worse. The Play is the only thing that provides "insurance of our sanity." Skip it even for a day, and the team might well tear itself apart. Lodge and Forester decide, therefore, that "the Play must go on" – despite their qualms about the consequences of having only eight characters, instead of nine.

It turns out that they needn't have worried – at least on that score. When the members of Life Team No. 3 resume the Play after Griffiths' death, they get a lot more than they bargained for. Despite Griffith's absence, all nine characters show up. What's more, the character created by Griffith turns out to be the Out-at-Elbows Philosopher, "the most self-assertive and dominant" of them all. How can the Philosopher play such a "prominent" role in the spectacle, despite his controller's absence? Gradually, the remaining audience members start to realize that their own characters are breaking free from them as well. It is quite horrifying, actually:

There was something wrong ... There was a certain mechanical wrongness, something out of place, a horrifying alienness that sent a shiver through you even when you couldn't spot the alienness.

This *wrongness* and *alienness* is that the characters of the Play have become sentient. Each of them has "drawn a little way apart ... cut the

apron strings ... stood on his [or her] own with the first dawning of independence." These fantasy figures are no longer just "mental puppets,"
enacting the impulses of the audience members who originally controlled them. Instead, each character has developed a will of his or
her own.

Even more alarmingly, these figures are no longer just virtual
reality images. They have emerged out of the screen, to stand instead
"on the stage, the little width of stage which ran before the screen."
They are just on the verge of walking over to meet their creators – and
show their independence from those creators. The characters in the
Play "were no longer projected imaginations – they were flesh and
blood."

This unexpected emergence, in all its irony, turns out to be the
"new approach" to creating life that the scientists of Life Team No.
3 have been fruitlessly seeking for so long. They have "failed at their
work and triumphed in their play." Forget all that anxiety and guilt,
all that endless "grubbing down" into the depths of being. There is
no longer any need to find a spark of life, or a hidden principle of
vitality. The hard problem of life simply dissolves (much as reductionist philosophers claim that the hard problem of consciousness
will dissolve, once we learn enough about the physiology and chemistry of the brain).

The lesson of the Play is that life can emerge full-blown, almost
anywhere. All you need is "the power of mind and electronic mys-
teries": that is to say, a whimsical imagination, amplified and
potentiated by sufficiently powerful computing technology. And of
course, as Clarke's Third Law tells us, "any sufficiently advanced technology is indistinguishable from magic." The more advanced and comprehensive the mediating machinery, the more these "new machines
are so clean and light" (to borrow a line from Donna Haraway's "Cyborg
Manifesto") as to be scarcely discernible, and the closer we come to
Lodge's ideal of "mind alone, without the aid of machines, without the
help of hands."

Lodge envisions a whole life-production industry, churning out
massive numbers of whatever "monsters" might be required:

To make a human monster you'd sit before a screen and you'd dream him up, bone by bone, hair by hair, brains, innards, special abilities and all. There'd be monsters by the billions to plant on those other planets. And the monsters would be human, for they'd be dreamed by brother humans working from a blueprint.

Nothing like this existed in 1953 (Simak 1953), when "Shadow Show" was written and published. But doesn't such an industry actually exist today? Simak's vision seems to foreshadow our current "creative industries," with their heavy use of computer-generated graphic design and animation. In the early twenty-first century, these technologies are thoroughly woven into the fabric of our work and our play alike. They can be used with equal efficacy to generate an architectural plan, a video sequence, an artifact for fabrication in a 3D printer, or a genetically modified life form. Everything is flexible and fluid; everything can be revised and reshaped pretty much at will. In other words, everything seems more or less alive. In the realm of what media theorist Deborah Levitt calls the *animatic apparatus*, "it doesn't so much matter what life is, but rather what you can do with it." We are currently witnessing

a reversal of the conventional direction of representation: instead of producing an image of an existing creature, we can produce a living being from an image. At the same time, images possess their own forms of vitality.

(Levitt 2018)

In this way, "Shadow Show" proposes a new sort of vitalism to replace the old one. For this new paradigm, there is no hidden secret of life, and no sharp distinction between life and nonlife. Instead, we have a universal process of *animation*. Liveliness is more or less present everywhere, albeit to differing degrees. Contemporary biology has no need for arcane secrets and novel physical laws. We no longer care about the metaphysical secret of life, but only about the pragmatic technology of fostering it. To quote Levitt once more, today "the reigning cultural paradigms of life" are shifting "in significant ways, moving away from questions about ontology, category, and being to ones of appearance, metamorphosis, and affect" (*The Animatic Apparatus*). Such is the "new approach" that emerges at the end of "Shadow Show," when the characters in the Play come so disconcertingly to life.

It is worth noting that Watson and Crick published their account of the structure of DNA in 1953, the same year as "Shadow Show." I have no idea if Simak was apprised of this development when he wrote his story. But the Watson-Crick discovery was the last nail in the coffin of the old vitalism, whose failure Simak so poignantly portrays. And it was also the first step of the ongoing revolution in molecular biology, which in tandem with high-powered computing led to the new vitalism of the "animatic apparatus" that informs our lives today, and that Simak's story so oddly envisages.

"Shadow Show" thus concludes by dissolving the hard problem of life with which it began. The mass production of "monsters" is now easily within our reach. But this inadvertent "triumph" of bioengineering does not erase the disquieting sense of *wrongness* that we feel as the roguish, disreputable, and comedically menacing characters of the Play emerge into the physical world. Despite "the bond of the created and creator," and despite the presumptive humanity of entities that have been "dreamed by brother humans working from a blueprint," the prospect of actual contact remains weird and uncanny and creepy. Lodge is understandably uneasy at the prospect of meeting his own character, the Rustic Slicker, with "his clodhopperish conceit [and] his smart-aleck snicker":

In just a little while the characters would step down off the stage and would mingle with them. And their creators? What would their creators do? Go screaming, raving mad?

What would he say to the Rustic Slicker?

What *could* he say to the Rustic Slicker?

And, more to the point, what would the Rustic Slicker have to say to him?

The story leaves us on the threshold of this new age of flexible production and animation. Lodge finds himself "unable to move, unable to say a word or cry out a warning, waiting for the moment when they would step down." Enmeshed as we are in the technologized folds of the new vitalism, paralysis seems a more appropriate response than self-congratulatory celebration.

Chapter 4
Dr. Franklin's Island

Dr. Franklin's Island (Halam 2002), a 2002 novel by Ann Halam (the pseudonym used by Gwyneth Jones for her young adult fiction), is described by the author as "sort of an argument with *The Island of Dr. Moreau*." The parallels between the two texts are clear enough. Halam's Dr. Franklin, like H. G. Wells' Dr. Moreau (Wells 1896), is a famous scientist who retreats to a distant island to do his research secretly, after being widely and publicly censured for controversial experiments that involved cruelty to animals. Both scientists are ruthlessly and singlemindedly determined to push through the species barrier that separates human beings from nonhuman animals. They do this work in spite of social taboos, and regardless of any risks, moral qualms, or actual harm to others. Both novels extrapolate from the science of their own times in order to question the ethics of scientific practice, and the powers and limits of what we define as "human."

In the course of her "argument" with Wells, Halam looks at many of the ways that biological theory and practice have changed in the more-than-century between his time and hers. *Dr. Franklin's Island* unfolds on the far side of the paradigm shift that Clifford Simak foresaw half a century earlier in "Shadow Show." This is most evident in the strategic inversion at the center of Halam's novel. Where Dr. Moreau struggles to mold animals into quasi-human beings, Dr. Franklin easily accomplishes the opposite. He subjects three British teenagers to transgenic experiments, transforming them against their will into human-animal hybrids. Semirah Garson, nicknamed Semi, the narrator, is made into a fish, something like a manta ray. Her friend Miranda Fallow is turned into "a big dark bird, big as an eagle, black as a raven." The third teenager, Arnie Pullman, becomes a long, thick snake.

The science depicted in *Dr. Franklin's Island* goes beyond anything we are actually able to do today. But Halam closely extrapolates from current trends. Twenty-first-century biotechnology is focused upon the programming and manufacture of genetically modified organisms (GMOs), transgenic hybrids, and even entirely artificial microbes. At the same time, scientists have increasingly become aware of the importance of horizontal (cross-species) gene transfer in the biological world. Bacteria share resistance to antibiotics in this way. Multicellular organisms use gene transfer as well. Recent studies have shown that both the mammalian placenta (Chuong 2013) and the mammalian long-term memory storage system (Pastuzyn 2018) have retroviral, extra-mammalian origins. For Wells, the modification and hybridization of distinct organisms was an extravagant fantasy; but Halam writes at a time when transgenesis is recognized as a scientific fact, and has almost become a technological commonplace.

Dr. Franklin's Island is also firmly anchored in the globalized neoliberal world that we inhabit today. No precise date is given, but nothing in the book – aside from Dr. Franklin's own procedures – goes beyond actually existing technologies and social structures. Media saturation is especially taken for granted. The novel begins, ironically enough, by recounting a stunt for reality television that goes wrong. Semi, Miranda, and Arnie are part of a group of "British Young Conservationists ... prizewinners in a competition run by the *Planet Savers* TV program." The teenagers are headed for "a wildlife conservation station deep in the Ecuador rain forest," where they will ostensibly help the scientists with "biodiversity experiment[s]," under the watchful eyes of the TV presenters and their cameras.

But the Young Conservationists never reach their destination. Their plane crashes over the ocean, and Semi, Miranda, and Arnie are the only survivors. They find themselves marooned on a distant island, which at first they think is unpopulated. They survive by gathering coconuts and spearing fish; they construct a shelter from palm fronds. It is important that, throughout their ordeal, the teens do not ever become feral and savage. This is not a *Lord of the Flies* scenario. It is true that Arnie is a bit obnoxious in a stereotypical nerdy teen boy way; he is a "big pale chunky boy" who has no friends and likes to pass the time by playing computer games. Alone on the island with two girls and no gaming consoles, he tends to be mean and sarcastic, and to do selfish things behind the others' backs. Nonetheless, underneath his "nasty and cynical" front, Arnie is really just another "lonely, misfit person." Most of the time, he works together with Semi and Miranda. The three teenagers do their best, not just to survive, but to recreate as much as possible of what they have lost. They do not have to start entirely from scratch, because they are able to make use of flotsam salvaged from the plane wreck. In this, they resemble the protagonists of such classic novels as *Robinson Crusoe* and *The Swiss Family Robinson* (the latter of which is explicitly mentioned in the text).

But it turns out that the island is far from being isolated and uninhabited. Like just about every other place in the world, it is in fact tightly connected to the global network and the global economy. The teenagers are watched from a distance all along, although they are unaware of this. Their Robinsonade comes to an end when first Arnie, and then Semi and Miranda, are captured and imprisoned by Dr. Franklin's paramilitary force. Arnie disappears from the narrative when he is separated from the others; it is only toward the end of the novel that the girls reestablish contact with him. For the most part, *Dr. Franklin's Island* recounts the growing friendship between Semi and Miranda, as they struggle to survive and escape from Dr. Franklin's cruelties.

Legally speaking, the island is Dr. Franklin's "private property," and the site of his research facility. Dr. Franklin regularly gets supplies, as well as workers, from the mainland, where he is "a big man ... the local *jefe*," with considerable financial and political influence. He is respected and deferred to, even though the details of his research are kept secret. Dr. Franklin thus remains connected to the world at large, in a way that Dr. Moreau does not.

Dr. Franklin also knows who the teens are, having been "in contact with the Search and Rescue operation" ever since the flight went down. Indeed, this is why he can get away with kidnapping them. He is sufficiently powerful and well-known that nobody will ever question his claim that he did not find the teenagers. "You are missing, believed dead," he and his flunky Dr. Skinner tell them; "you don't exist" as far as the rest of the world is concerned. Semi and her friends have no recourse; instead of becoming junior experimenters, they are made into experiments themselves.

Hallam says in an interview that, when she reread *The Island of Dr. Moreau*, she especially disliked "H. G. Wells' ideas about animal nature versus human nature." Wells' vision is grounded in a pernicious dualism. Human transcendence remains forever in tension with crass, raging animal drives: what Dr. Moreau calls "cravings, instincts, desires that harm humanity." Wells, like so many other Victorians, gives a Darwinian twist to the old Platonic and Christian vision of human beings split between angel and beast, or rationality and animality. Dr. Moreau's goal is to liquidate this duality, so that only pure reason remains. His torturous vivisections of various animals are intended to extirpate their bestial nature, and raise them up to fully human status:

Each time I dip a living creature into the bath of burning pain, I say, "This time I will burn out all the animal; this time I will make a rational creature of my own!"

But of course, Dr. Moreau never succeeds in doing this. He is no better at playing God than Victor Frankenstein was. For all the tortures that Dr. Moreau inflicts, and despite endowing his animals with the power of speech, he is unable to reach "the seat of the emotions," which is where the real resistance to rationality lies. After completing his surgeries, therefore, Dr. Moreau finds that he still needs to subject his Beast Folk to harsh and continual discipline. He sees this as the only way to keep them more or less human. At any opportunity, Dr. Moreau complains, "they revert. As soon as my hand is taken from them the beast begins to creep back, begins to assert itself again."

Wells gives us a gruesome portrait of Dr. Moreau's excessive rationalism, and of the underlying sadism that drives it. But Dr. Moreau's governance of his island also works as a hyperbolic example – or a parody – of the nineteenth-century regime of *biopower*. Michel Foucault describes biopower as a set of "techniques for achieving the subjugation of bodies and the control of populations" (Foucault 1976). In the new power arrangements that arise in Europe over the course of the nineteenth century, discipline does not just constrain actual behavior; it gets extended to all "the basic biological features of the human species" (Foucault 2007).

In other words, biopower is not just about *what you do*; more crucially, it is focused on policing *what you are*. Biopower is all about a normative model of what it means to be human. Dr. Moreau tries to keep the Beast Folk human by continually chastising and haranguing them, by forcing them to perform incessant rituals, and by repeatedly threatening them with pain. This is Foucault's disciplinary society *par excellence*. We might say that Wells literalizes the presuppositions and mechanisms of biopower, by giving us a story in which actual animals are tortured in order to fit them within rigid constraints of what it means to be human.

Dr. Moreau's forcible humanization of his animals is continually shadowed by its inverse: his panic about the *reversion* of his creatures to their original bestial nature. This fear of reversion is a central feature of nineteenth- and twentieth-century Euro-American racism. Humanity is defined according to a normative model: white, male, heterosexual, and Protestant, and therefore supposedly "rational." Anyone not conforming to this model is regarded as irrational and less than fully human. So-called "scientific racism" is the underside of the regime of biopower. Later speculative writers in this tradition become even more unhinged than Wells' Dr. Moreau, in their dread of a supposed animalistic reversion that threatens to undermine the privileges of white humanity. H. P. Lovecraft writes whole stories in this vein, like "The Shadow Over Innsmouth" and "The Call of Cthulhlu," in the latter of which he channels *The Island of Dr. Moreau* directly:

There are vocal qualities peculiar to men, and vocal qualities peculiar to beasts; and it is terrible to hear the one when the source should yield the other.

Things are altogether different in the world of *Dr. Franklin's Island.* Obviously, racism and misogyny have far from disappeared from twenty-first century life; if anything, they are on the rise in today's political climate. Nonetheless, contemporary biology does not recognize any sharp distinction between different human types, let alone between humanity and animality, or between rationality and emotion. These all come down to matters of degree, rather than differences of kind. Genes work in the same ways across all living species. There is no hierarchical chain of being, but only a *mesh* (as Timothy Morton calls it: Morton 2010) of interconnected and mutually dependent entities. Where Dr. Moreau wishes to extirpate animal-being, therefore, Dr. Franklin rather desires to capture it, appropriate it, and capitalize upon it. Far from seeking to transcend animality, Dr. Franklin regards animals – or more precisely, their genomes – as valuable resources, available to him for selection, manipulation, and productive use.

All this is possible because Dr. Franklin directly works on the genotype, whereas Dr. Moreau only works on the level of gross anatomy, or of what we now call the phenotype. (Part of the point here is that the very distinction between genotype and phenotype had not yet been recognized when Wells wrote his novel.) Where Dr. Moreau's approach is physiological, Dr. Franklin's is genetic. Dr. Moreau assaults and alters animal bodies on the largest scale; Dr. Franklin rearranges things on the molecular level. Dr. Moreau relies upon "the plasticity of living forms," and seeks, through vivisection, "to find out the extreme limit of plasticity in a living shape." In this way, he is more a precursor of D'Arcy Thompson than a follower of Darwin. In contrast, Dr. Franklin is a true heir of Watson and Crick; he invokes the power of DNA in order to direct and alter biological growth. Semi and Miranda are not subjected to invasive surgery; instead, they are treated with infusions and injections made from their own stem cells, "cut and spliced" with "pieces of original animal genes" as well as with entirely new artificial genes "that had never existed before in the world."

Dr. Franklin's experiments reflect the way that the new biology of the twenty-first century is, above all, pragmatic and operational: concerned with fostering performance, rather than with capturing essence. Sophia Roosth observes in her recent study of synthetic biology that the aim of contemporary research is "not experiment but manufacture, not reduction but construction, not analysis but synthesis." If a software model does not accurately reflect the activity of a virus, for instance, synthetic biologists respond "not [by] reprogramming the software model but [by] rebuilding the physical virus *to conform to the software model*" (Roosth 2017). Genomes are tailored to fit whatever purposes we want them to serve. Contemporary biology is constructivist and performative; that is to say, its premises are diametrically opposed to those of nineteenth-century biopower. Identity is irrelevant; actual activity is everything. Today's biotechnology is not concerned with what life *is*, or with any supposed essence of humanity, but only with – as Deleuze puts it, paraphrasing Spinoza – *what a body can do.*

In this performative, operational way, contemporary biotechnology is still (or again) a sort of vitalistic practice. But this is not the old vitalism. As I already have argued in reference to Simak's "Shadow Show," our current sense of vital animacy is radically different from the vitalism of the nineteenth and early twentieth centuries. Today, we no longer need to posit anything like Victor Frankenstein's mysterious "spark of life." For we now understand that vital transformation is a common, everyday process. It is entirely explicable in physicochemical terms, and therefore it is as mundane as it is magical. As Semi says, reflecting on her own transgenic crossings,

Have you ever seen a seedling, a baby weed, shoving up from under a concrete slab? Or pushing through to the sunlight, through four or five centimeters of tarmac? That's what changing was like for me ... That's the power that Dr. Franklin had put into his DNA infusions. That's what the chemistry of life can do.

The "chemistry of life" is active nearly everywhere on our planet. And it works in the same way in Dr. Franklin's extreme transgenic experiments as it does in the ordinary growth and reproduction of living things. This is why, as Dr. Franklin puts it at one point, "the idea of growing a new kind of human being from scratch [i]s a nonstarter." Victor Frankenstein was entirely misguided. You can get much better results, Dr. Franklin says, by "putting new genes into a ready-made living human body, and getting it to change." Rather than worrying about how dead, inert matter can be endowed with life, Dr. Franklin seeks to induce smooth, lateral, and seamlessly reversible metamorphoses among multiple already-living entities. With his transgenic technology, he hopes to achieve, for bioengineering, something like the "universal transmutability of fluctuation" that Melinda Cooper sees at work "in the circulation of capital today" (Cooper 2010).

Dr. Franklin's experiments incorporate a high degree of uncertainty into their basic operations, much as actual pharmaceutical research projects do – and as financial derivatives do as well. As Miranda remarks to Semi at one point,

Transgenic experiments can be random. I don't think they knew *how* we would turn out. That's the whole point of being a scientist, isn't it? You try things, to see what happens.

This is why the old biopower, which sought to enforce norms decreed in advance, is obsolete. Today instead, biotechnology and finance alike reject pregiven forms, and seek instead to adaptively manage future uncertainties. As Cooper puts it, power now works through rhizomatic proliferation and variation:

The power of leverage is one of potentiation through connection, the power to liquefy and freeze relations, to potentialize and depotentialize connections, and thus to shape (and be shaped by) the possibilities of movement of everyday life. This is a power that operates in the future subjunctive, since the promise of leverage is a claim over the future in all its unknowability – a claim over event worlds that have yet to actualize in space and time.

(Cooper 2010)

Cooper is writing about "leverage" in financial markets; but her logic applies with equal force to the transformations wrought by postgenomic biotechnology. The "chemistry of life," as embodied in DNA, is at once manipulable and unpredictable. DNA can be programmed like a computer; nonetheless, the consequences of this programming are nonlinear and not entirely within the programmers' control. DNA molecules are tightly organized, in chains that can reach great length; and these chains tend to strongly conserve their organization. But at the same time, thanks to its modular structure, DNA is also highly amenable to mutation and rearrangement. These characteristics underlie the *animacy* of life as we understand it today. Transgenic technology operates in the mode of what Cooper calls the "future subjunctive": it remains open to, and is able to profit from, a wide range of possible situations. The "chemistry of life" exhibits the "flexibility and adaptability" that are central to what Luc Boltanski and Eve Chiapello describe as "the new spirit of capitalism" in the twenty-first century (Boltanski and Chiapello 2018). Life today is cheap: plentiful, easily manipulable, and just as easily disposable.

It comes as no surprise, therefore, that Dr. Franklin is a very different sort of "mad scientist" figure than Dr. Moreau. Wells' character is megalomaniacal in his ambitions and tormented by his repeated failures; he seems to revel in the infliction of pain. Dr. Franklin is equally megalomaniacal, and is in fact described as a "mad scientist" by Semi at several points in the text. But Dr. Franklin, unlike Dr. Moreau, is always cold and detached, with a "creepy beaming smile." Semi notes that Dr. Franklin is "never nasty," and always "polite." He promises the teenagers that he "will cause as little physical pain as possible. I am never needlessly cruel!" Of course, what he means by this is only that he does not revel in cruelty for its own sake. He wants his research to move forward efficiently, and he is only cruel to the extent that this serves his research goals. Despite the leveling power of his new technologies, he is still committed to the old scientific goal of humanity's absolute domination of nature. This fits in with his megalomania, since he regards "everyone but himself" as "still an animal, a thing to be used," and therefore as expendable. Indeed, Semi observes that Dr. Franklin treats her and Miranda in much the same way that "normal people treat normal animals, a lot of the time": we lock them up and exploit them, compelling them to do precisely what we want, "and yet we somehow expect them to *like* us."

Where Dr. Moreau is tormented by the continuing failures of his experiments, Dr. Franklin is calmly "prepared to sacrifice" his experimental subjects whenever he needs to. "Of course there's a price to pay" for any research advance; just as in the derivatives market, unpredictability and failure are built in to the project from the very beginning. Indeed, Dr. Franklin, like a derivatives trader, thrives on uncertainty. He regards each research setback as a new opportunity to exercise his mastery. When things go wrong with an experiment, he says that "I don't look on this as a failure ... It has been a very exciting first trial." He is sarcastically delighted whenever Semi and Miranda try to escape or otherwise resist him: "Many congratulations!" he tells them; "Excellent! Well done!" The girls' unexpected behavior confirms the animacy and flexibility of biological matter – the very qualities that Dr. Franklin seeks to cultivate. Every act of disobedience is a new source of experimental data for him, or a stress test allowing him to debug and refine his procedures. Dr. Franklin praises Semi and Miranda for being "highly resourceful, psychologically very resilient," which makes them "excellent candidates for my first human trials."

Semi is rightly disturbed when she hears this sort of praise:

"Resilient?" I repeated. It wasn't that I didn't understand the word, it was because I couldn't understand why these compliments sounded so creepy.

The creepiness has to do, I would suggest, with the way that *resilience* has become a neoliberal buzzword. Where Dr. Moreau fears the moment when "the beast begins to creep back, begins to assert itself again," Dr. Franklin considers Semi's and Miranda's most valuable trait to be precisely that they are able to "bounce back ... You don't crawl into a corner whimpering when you're faced with a tremendous challenge. You deal with it." As John Patrick Leary observes, *resilience* is a key concept for neoliberalism because, at the same time that it praises "one's own, private ability to bounce back from hardship," it also takes such hardship as a given: "one can only be 'resilient to crisis' – or, more to the point, expect others to be – if one first accepts crisis as a more or less regular condition of those others' existence" (Leary 2018).

Consequently, as Robin James puts it, resilience discourse means that victimized and oppressed people "are individually responsible for overcoming" the very damage that has been systematically and concertedly inflicted upon them (James 2015). Dr. Franklin praises Semi and Miranda for having what it takes to endure the abuse he subjects them to, and also for providing him with new challenges along the way. This is quite different from the more straightforward sadism of Dr. Moreau's vivisections – though I hesitate to judge which is worse.

Along with all of this, Dr. Franklin also offers Semi and Miranda the "choice" as to which one of them will be transformed into a bird, and which into a fish. They are "free to make" the choice, whichever way they prefer. This gives us a gruesomely hilarious illustration of how *rational choice* works in the neoliberal order. Every individual is "free to choose" (as Milton Friedman liked to say: Friedman and Friedman 1980) among various alternatives. But the alternatives themselves are severely constrained, already given in advance, and never in the individual's control. Dr. Franklin tells Semi and Miranda that there are "very good technical reasons" as to which animals he proposes to turn them into. Their "free choice" does not include selecting a different species, let alone being able to avoid the transformation altogether.

It is also worth noting that Dr. Franklin does not transform any of the teenagers into other mammals, but only into less closely related creatures (birds, reptiles, fish – at least they still remain vertebrates). In other words, Dr. Franklin does not just dehumanize Semi, Miranda, and Arnie; he *de-mammalizes* them as well. Turning them into dogs or tigers, or even into rats or pigs, would presumably not be alien and alienating enough.

Unlike Dr. Moreau, who works in solitude, Dr. Franklin has a large staff of collaborators and assistants – or better, employees – as befits the cost and complexity of biological research today. The island is not an isolated outpost, so much as it is an "evil paradise" (Davis and Monk 2011): a fully functioning authoritarian mini-state, with its own particular role to play in the neoliberal world order. Dr. Franklin's staff includes "orderlies and technicians" and armed security guards, not to mention the people who clean and cook and take care of supplies.

These workers all live on the island with their families, in what is essentially a company town (a relic of nineteenth-century capitalism that is making a comeback today: cf. Richman 2018, and Straus and Zamfira 2017). Miranda refers sarcastically at one point to what she imagines as "Dr. Franklin's Island General Stores."

Dr. Franklin's research facility is nothing like Dr. Moreau's "House of Pain" – or for that matter, Victor Frankenstein's "workshop of filthy creation." Rather, Dr. Franklin's compound is large, self-contained, sanitized, and sterile. In contemporary biotechnology, as Donna Haraway puts it, "the new machines are so clean and light" (Haraway 1991). Dr. Franklin's laboratory consists of "empty, bright, clinical rooms," all of which are fully climate controlled. Some of these rooms are reminiscent of hotel suites, while others are more like prison cells. In every room, supplies are neatly stockpiled in "walk-in cold cupboard[s] with stacked shelves." Desks are piled with computer keyboards and monitors – rather than with anything like Dr. Moreau's gruesome surgical tools. Video spy cameras are everywhere. Doors are always locked, and operated by codes tapped out on keypads. Here, as more generally in what Deleuze calls "control societies" (Deleuze 1995), crude force is replaced by discreet but uninterrupted surveillance, and a continual *modulation* of effects.

Dr. Franklin begins his experiments, just as Dr. Moreau does, by endowing other animals with human traits. His odd menagerie includes such specimens as bats with human legs, pigs who have human hands and who "squealed and chattered at each other, in high-pitched almost childish voices," a capybara with "puffy and red" human lips, and "something that looked like a monkey head with octopus tentacles." But producing such disturbing and incongruous hybrids is not a goal in itself. Such experiments are only "steps on the way to a much greater goal ... we've gone beyond them now." Where Dr. Moreau seeks to humanize beasts, Dr. Franklin and Dr. Skinner don't see this as a sufficiently ambitious goal. They proclaim that "we've gone as far as we can, infusing human genetic material into dumb animals." Evidently their transgenic technology does not lead them to reject human species chauvinism. Rather, they seem to hyperbolize it. Dr. Franklin and Dr. Skinner are desperate to *go further*, to take the "next step": to remake people so that they become "more than human" or "superhumans."

Dr. Franklin therefore pontificates about growth, discovery, and entrepreneurial initiative – in striking contrast to Dr. Moreau's language of rationality and moral regeneration. As experimental subjects, Semi and Miranda will "serve the cause of human progress ... Look on it as a great adventure." Indeed, Dr. Franklin sounds at times like a Silicon Valley entrepreneur, drunk on his own vision:

See if you can picture some of the possibilities. Imagine being as strong as an elephant. Imagine being able to use sunshine to make food, like a plant. Imagine being able to fly like a bird. Imagine being able to breathe underwater, and swim with the fishes. Imagine ... though this is farther off, I admit ... being able to breathe different gases, or live comfortably in the hard vacuum of space.

(ellipses in original)

All of these are familiar staples of transhumanist speculation, not to mention science fiction. Nonetheless, Dr. Franklin's exalted language cannot be taken at face value. Like so much entrepreneurial discourse, it is largely hype. Though Dr. Franklin does endow Semi with the ability to breathe underwater, and Miranda with the ability to fly, these changes do not really *enhance* the girls' abilities; they just replace one set of capacities with another. Semi-the-fish is able to breathe underwater, but at the price of no longer being able to breathe air. Miranda-the-bird has wings, but they have replaced those crucial human organs, the arms and hands. Dr. Franklin, it turns out, is less interested in the "science fiction" of superhuman abilities and "interplanetary travel" than he is in coming up with a solid "commercial proposition." His real aim is to improve his transgenic formula to the point where he can sell it

to an exotic holiday company ... Imagine it. You take a pill, or a couple of injections. Like being vaccinated. They put you in a flotation tank overnight, while the ugly stuff is going on. You wake up in a five-star underwater hotel, on your ocean safari. Or in some kind of luxury cliffside flying lodge, on the wall of the Grand Canyon. Spend two weeks exploring the deep ocean, or flying like a bird, then go through the same thing in reverse.

This is one of the novel's most brilliant ironies. Dr. Franklin is not really trying to surpass or transcend the human condition – at least not in the short run. Rather, he wants to realize a business plan. It is not surprising, therefore, that Semi and Miranda feel cheated once they have undergone Dr. Franklin's treatment. The girls find, to their disappointment, that they have been turned into "monsters, not superhumans." They retain just enough of their humanity to be able to realize that animal traits have overwritten, rather than augmented, their human ones. Now they are less than human, or other than merely human – and this is not the same as being "more than human."

In depicting these changes, Halam rejects Wells' creaky Victorian dualism, and draws instead upon an older tradition: the Romantic celebration of animal unselfconsciousness. This is arguably more in line with our current understanding of our own animality. As Halam puts it in her interview, the novel seeks to express

the wonder and joy of being reunited with the animal kingdom, rediscovering the delight of being an animal, at home in the living world – but still this special kind of *self-aware, conscious* animal that is a human being.

A human being may well be a "special kind" of animal, but we remain animals nonetheless. We may well be distinguished by our strange capacity for self-awareness and self-alienation; but we are not regressing, or losing something essential, when we feel the embodied enjoyment of being, like our fellow creatures, "at home in the living world." Despite the horrors of their imprisonment, and the pain of the transformation itself, Semi and Miranda are able to positively enjoy their new animal status. This is because, like Shelley's skylark or Keats' nightingale, they are able to put aside their human self-consciousness along with their human bodily forms:

Before the change, we'd have thought that losing our human feelings, becoming mutant-monsters in our *minds* would have been the worst horror imaginable. In fact it turns out to be the only thing that makes life possible ... there's no disgust and horror at being monsters.

Now that Semi is a fish, her new bodymind affords her new sorts of perceptions, and new powers to affect and to be affected. Semi feels a true happiness in discovering all the things that her fish-body can do, and in exercising her new powers to the fullest. Being an animal turns out to be easy:

One very good thing is that we don't have to make any effort to be our animal selves. Miranda-the-bird and Semi-the-fish know everything they need to know. They eat, sleep, move, react like the animals they are. All we have to do is learn to sort of keep our human thoughts out of the way, and everything just happens.

The human thoughts never entirely disappear, but it is not hard to push them into the background. In Semi's fish state, she no longer has to deal with her feelings of awkwardness and anxiety, her perpetual sense of inadequacy, and her shyness: all the trials and tribulations that have afflicted her as a teenager (and that are described in excruciating detail in the opening pages of the novel, before Semi's life is changed by the plane crash). Instead, Semi feels entirely at home in her animal body, which is also, immediately, her mind:

My head wasn't separate from my body anymore. My head and my heart were together, in the center of me, and *me* was this smooth, flowing delta-plane ... my legs weren't dangling extra things anymore, they were *inside me* as well ... my whole body responded. I went flying forward, backward, up, down, with perfect control, any direction I wanted. I was free, so free.

This delta body, with its reabsorption of extremities (head and limbs) into one central mass, corresponds to a psychical reabsorption of mind into immediate physical experience. Everything is "inside me," Semi says, and her ability to flow through the water in three dimensions is unimpeded. Semi describes the sheer rapture of swimming as a manta ray as

the most magical experience of my life ... Everything was alive. The water was full of movement, sound and light. I try to think of how it felt in human terms, and the nearest I can come is ... it was like swimming through music. Not loud, wild, music, not that night, but sparkling, dancing music, with a deep steady underbeat, and distant voices weaving in and out; and I was part of this music ... *Joy*, that's the only word for it.

Such is the beautiful potential of transgenic transformation. "What do animals do with themselves all day?" Semi asks herself. And she immediately answers: "A lot of nothing, basically." But this is a joyous and relaxing nothing: positive and restful, without any sense of emptiness or lack. Dr. Franklin has not only undermined Dr. Moreau's binary opposition between human and animal; he has also dismantled Cartesian skepticism, with its concomitant dualism of mind and body. The wonder of animal-being is that consciousness and body plan run together, in Spinozian parallel. As Semi reflects at one point,

I think animals without hands have different minds from animals with hands. Animals with hands that they can use to pick things up – like monkeys, humans, birds, mice, rats – tend to like being busy, and tinkering with things. Animals without hands, like snakes, or fish, or cats, are happy doing nothing for long periods. I'd always been a thoughtful person. As a fish, I completely shared the daydreamer-animal attitude to life.

Semi and Miranda find that it is difficult to think human thoughts, let alone express them, when you have the physiology of a fish or a bird. In her fish form, Semi is no longer physically able to speak, or to make any sort of noise, since her lungs and larynx have been transformed into other organs. However, she still retains the *capacity* for human language and thought, since she still possesses human DNA, and the specifically human portions of her brain. To accommodate this, Dr. Franklin implants "microchips in [the teenagers'] brains, little tiny radios connected to [their] speech centers," allowing them to converse via what he calls "radio telepathy." This is a sort of virtual reality simulation. The girls find themselves in a "white place," something "like being inside a cloud." There is no background, no "world," to anchor this virtual experience: "everywhere you actually *looked* at the whiteness, it blurred out, and vanished into nothingness." But in this virtual nonspace, the girls "can see mental images of each other" and hear each other's speech.

Semi finds the experience of "radio telepathy" unnerving, not just due to the lack of any background, but also because

I had the weirdest feeling of being in two places at once. I knew that while I sat with Miranda there, the mutant-fish monster that was also me was still swimming around in that pool.

The two states of hybrid being – human and animal – both continue to exist, but they do not coincide or fuse together. You can experience things either animalistically or humanly, but you cannot have both sorts of experience at the same time. Instead, you can move from one framework to the other by "flipp[ing] some mental switches." Miranda suggests to Semi that "it's like having dual nationality. You're officially two people, but you don't feel anything odd." The girls are unable to reconcile or combine their dual natures; but by moving back and forth between them, they are able to revel in a sort of Nietzschean perspectivism. They contemplate each condition from the point of view of the other one:

In my dual-nationality mind, it was as if I *remembered* everything that a natural-born tropical manta ray would know. Only better than remembering, because this wasn't like Semi-the-girl remembering facts she'd learned, and sometimes getting them wrong. It was certain knowledge, like knowing the difference between light and dark. These "memories" must have come from the fish DNA that had been grafted into my human DNA. But because I was girl as well as fish, I could think about my inbuilt animal knowledge with a human mind. I really enjoyed that.

This art of inverting perspectives is the crucial lesson of *Dr. Franklin's Island*. Semi and Miranda are able to fully enjoy their animal condition at one moment, and to fight against the coercion that led to it in the next. Swimming in her pool, Semi confesses to having "the strangest feeling that we could live like this, and be fairly content" in animal form, pretty much indefinitely. She finds her animal powers "amazing." She immediately adds a qualification, however: "if only we weren't prisoners ... But we are prisoners."

The novel asks us to entertain both sides of this dilemma. Dr. Franklin performs his transgenic surgery because he wants to capture and commodify animal experience. If he can produce it on demand, in a reliable, objective, easily manageable form, then he can sell it as an exotic holiday package. The privatization and marketing of aspects of life that were previously open and common – and especially of such impalpable qualities as experiences, atmospheres, and moods – is one of the frontiers of contemporary neoliberal capitalism. And the operationalism of mainstream biotechnology is largely oriented toward this goal.

But at the same time, Dr. Franklin's ambitions are thwarted, because the teenagers' animal rapture remains opaque to him. He cannot grasp or measure it, no matter how thoroughly he works to "biopsy the internal organs and the brain, take samples of your spinal fluid," and so on. "I could see [Dr. Franklin's] frustration," Semi says at the moment of their final confrontation:

He had made us, but he didn't know what was going on in our minds ... That was what frightened him. Not Miranda's talons or Arnie's massive strength. He'd created us, but he didn't understand us, and for him that was unbearable.

This is the hope that resonates through Halam's otherwise distressing tale. At the end of the novel, Semi, Miranda, and Arnie manage to kill Dr. Franklin, escape from his island, obtain their antidotes, return to human form, and be reunited with their parents. But at the end of the novel, and of their story, they know that they have not really come "back to normal," even if they "look almost normal on the outside." For

Whatever we look like on the outside, there's something we all three know. *We are not back to the way we were before.* Once you've been made transgenic, you stay transgenic. The different DNA is lurking in our cells.

Semi, Miranda, and Arnie still retain the potential for meta-morphosis, a power lurking deep within their cells. And given their experiences, perhaps they feel that being "normal" isn't much more attractive than being the prisoner of a mad scientist was. Semi recalls feeling, when she first became a fish,

as if being normal had been a straitjacket, and this was how it felt when all the horrible restraints, that you'd been suffering all your life without realizing it, were magically taken away.

Such a feeling could never be that of an actual manta ray, whose fishiness is the only condition it knows. It could also never be that of a human being who lives an entirely commodified existence, never venturing beyond the limits of normalcy. Rather, *Dr. Franklin's Island* is the dream of a transgenic being, a human-become-fish-become-human hybrid entity. The novel expresses this dream and this beauty, at the same time that it recounts the terror of a technoscience that seeks absolute domination, and that instrumentally treats human and animal beings only as "experimental subjects."

That is why *Dr. Franklin's Island* ends with a coda, in which Semi continues to think about her transgenic potential:

I know that we can transform again. I believe it will happen, some way, somehow. I think about breathing water and swimming through the music of the ocean. I think about having a skeleton of supple cartilage instead of brittle bone. I think about feeling my whole body as one soaring, gliding, sweeping wing. I know that Miranda will never forget being able to fly. I dream of another planet, with an ocean of heavy air, where I can swim and she can fly, where we can be the marvelous creatures that we became; and be free, together, with no bars between us. I wonder if it exists, somewhere, out there ...

Chapter 5
Message in a Bottle

Nalo Hopkinson's 2005 short story "Message in a Bottle" is a fable about art, communication, and futurity. It was originally written for *Futureways*, a multi-authored volume described by its editors as

a faux science fiction novel ... *Futureways* is the story of an art exhibition in the distant future, the biennale of a future civilization ... each chapter deals with the transport of art objects to the venue of the biennale, a task difficult enough in the modern era but even more tenuous in the imagined futures of the writers.

(McBride and Rubsamen 2005)

Hopkinson later republished the story in two of her own collections: first in the chapbook *Report from Planet Midnight* (Hopkinson 2012), and then in her short story compendium *Falling in Love With Hominids* (Hopkinson 2015). As these republications suggest, "Message in a Bottle" is legible outside of the occasion for which it was initially written. Indeed, although the story ultimately concerns "the transport of art objects" into the distant future for an exhibition, it tells us very little about this presumptive future. Instead, it is recognizably set in something like the present moment. The prompt for the story suggests a movement through space ("transport ... to the venue") unfolding in an "imagined future" time. Most of the stories in the *Futureways* anthology follow this conceit (though little attempt is made to place all the stories in a common future world, or to have the same future art exhibition as the destination for all of them). But Hopkinson inverts the entire premise. She imagines the difficulties of transport through time instead of through space, and she evokes a strange, distant future only in terms of the ways that, via time travel, it reveals itself in advance to us in the present.

Indeed, the notion of a future art exhibition is only mentioned explicitly at the very end of "Message in a Bottle" – though it then becomes apparent that this prospect has structured everything in the story from the beginning. The retrospective narrative structure gives the story an odd, shifting emotional tone. For most of my first reading, "Message in a Bottle" seemed light and humorous. Then, when I got to the end, I was thrown for a loop – because things had suddenly turned weird and outrageous. It was only on rereading the story that I grasped how twisted and distressing the situation it describes really is. "Message in a Bottle" sneaks up on you, and leaves a disturbing aftertaste.

If the story at first seems cute and funny, this is largely due to the charm of its protagonist-narrator Greg. He is an installation artist, living in present-day St. John's, Newfoundland. He identifies himself as a heterosexual man of Indigenous origins. His friends and lovers tend also to be nonwhite people, like his "lush and brown" girlfriend Cecilia. Greg is insightful and conscious about racial and post-colonial issues, and the politics of art and culture; though perhaps less so about gender and sexuality.

Greg explains his cultural politics by telling us about

this bunch of Sioux activists, how they'd been protesting against a university whose archaeology department had dug up one of their ancestral burial sites ... When the director of the department refused to reconsider, these guys had gone one night to the graveyard where his great-grandmother was buried. They'd dug up her remains, laid out all the bones, labelled them with little tags. They did jail time, but the university returned their ancestors' remains to the band council.

The action was effective, in other words, even though the activists paid a price for it. The white archaeologists were forced to acknowledge the gross asymmetry between how they treat the cultural values and material traces of other (supposedly "ancient") peoples, and how they treat their own. What deserves reverence, and what can be taken as mere data for analysis? Why do archaeologists and anthropologists consider some groups of people to be "primitive," even though we are all living in the same highly technologized present moment? Greg's anecdote recalls the actual case of Kenniwick Man, a 9,000-year-old skeleton dug up by archaeologists in 1996, subjected to multiple tests, and only returned to the Umatilla people for proper burial in 2017 (Thomas 2000).

Greg's own gallery installation, "The Excavations," which he describes in the course of the story, is about the social roles played by physical *stuff*. It takes the form of a mock archaeological site. Greg packs the art gallery with "half a ton of dirt," in which he buries such objects as "a rubber boot" that has been cast aside by the person who wore it, "a large plastic jug that used to hold bleach, and that had been refitted as a bucket for a small child to tote water in," and "a scrap of hand-woven blanket with brown stains on it." When visitors enter the gallery, they "get basic excavation tools. When they pull something free of the soil, it triggers a story about the artifact on the monitors above." The exhibition thus calls our attention to "the kinds of present-day historical artifacts" that actual archaeologists "[toss] aside in their zeal to get at the iconic past of the native peoples" they are studying.

In this way, Greg's installation undermines notions of the ahistorical authenticity of Indigenous peoples, such as well-meaning white Westerners are all too likely to project upon them. It points out – just as the Sioux activists' action did – how Indigenous peoples, no less than white Westerners, inhabit the same present moment; and that this present itself is deeply historical, inflected by the intertwined histories of all the peoples involved in it. That is to say, the lived and experienced present, no less than the reconstructed past, is deeply contingent, embedded in stories and processes, and open to contestation and change.

In "The Excavations," Greg acquaints his viewers with the actual, present-day material culture of the Indigenous people of (in this case) Chiapas, Mexico. The exhibition shows how this culture is multiple and heterogeneous, and how it is rich in meanings despite economic poverty. This living culture bears the traces both of colonialist oppression and of the native people's resistance to this oppression. Indigenous peoples, with their histories, their political struggles, and their values, must be seen as actors in the present. We cannot relegate them (as anthropologists all too often have done) to the status of human relics, stuck in ways of living that belong to the past.

The installation itself is self-consciously shaped by the historical contingencies of its own creation. Greg notes that the soil he uses for the exhibition is

left over from a local archaeological dig. I wish I could have gotten it directly from Mexico, but I couldn't afford the permit for doing that.

This reminds us that art-making is not just pure and unfettered expression. For it is never free from economic, legal, and bureaucratic constraints. But even the artifacts in the installation that actually do come from Chiapas do not simply "speak for themselves." Objects are shaped and given meaning by the ways that they have been used, and by the narratives that take them up. We can only really understand an artifact when we grasp its history and its context. We need to know who wore that particular boot, and what was carried in that particular plastic jug. Now, any use to which an object is put leaves traces behind on the object itself. But these traces are generally incomplete and fragmentary. The challenge of archaeology is to reconstruct a fuller history from the insufficient traces that it leaves behind. This is always a difficult, perilous act of interpretation. It's an uncertain and unfinishable task in both directions. On the one hand, an object, in its palpable physical presence (*this* plastic boot, *this* stained fragment of blanket), is always more that the stories that can be told about it. But on the other hand, and at the same time, these stories extend beyond what any particular artifact can ever contain; they encompass more of the world than what is immediately present.

This doubleness is expressed in the very shape of Greg's installation, which pairs material artifacts with video clips that tell their stories. Neither half of the exhibition would work without the other. It is equally important that we actually *find* these physical objects by digging them out of the soil, and that we learn the stories of their provenance and their many transformations. "The Excavations" is a complex *assemblage*, networking cheap technologies (boots, buckets, and blankets) with expensive ones (computers, video monitors, and digital recordings), physical objects with streams of images and sounds, Mexican artifacts with Canadian replicas, and objects that work to tell stories with objects about which the stories are told. The installation also points up its own inevitable incompleteness; however much we get from it, we must also realize that there is always *more*. For this reason, not everything in the exhibition is given an explanatory narrative. Greg has carefully "videotaped every artifact with which I'd seeded the soil that went onto the gallery floor," but "some of the artifacts are 'blanks' that trigger no stories" on the video monitors.

Greg's personal life, like his art, is inflected by his experiences as a nonwhite man in a racist society. He is proud of his Indigenous heritage, but he rejects the clichés that white people all too frequently believe about what the life of a person with that heritage is supposed to be like. For instance, even though Greg covers his installation in half a ton of soil, he is far from being a traditionalist whose primary tie is to the land. Rather, Greg is a techie, an urbanite, and sex-positive. He and Cecilia "geekspeak at each other all the time. When we're out in public, people fall silent in linguistic bafflement around us." He gleefully tells us how he and Cecilia will go "shopping for a new motherboard" in the morning, then "hump like bunnies till we both come screaming" in the afternoon.

Greg also describes himself as something of a *bricoleur* (though he doesn't actually use this word). He gathers all sorts of miscellaneous stuff, and ends up using it for his art. Indeed, he is really a hoarder; he accumulates and keeps whatever odds and ends and pieces of junk he happens to find:

My home is also my studio, and it's a warren of tangled cables, jury-rigged networked computers, and piles of books about as stable as playing-card houses. Plus bins full of old newspaper clippings, bones of dead animals, rusted metal I picked up on the street, whatever. I don't throw anything away if it looks the least bit interesting. You never know when it might come in handy as part of an installation piece. The chaos has a certain nestlike comfort to it.

I think that Greg's sense of "nestlike comfort" is the key here. His accumulations, with their mild but not unmanageable disorder, make for a relaxing sense of repletion. This offers a sharp contrast to the uptight, obsessive neatness of normative white bourgeois suburban life. No matter what physical object Greg needs, he is likely to be able to find it somewhere or other, in one of his piles of stuff. The "chaos" that always surrounds him marks his home as being really *his*. He finds it familiar and relaxing, all the more so in that outsiders cannot make heads or tails of it.

There is one vitally important thing I haven't mentioned yet. This is that Greg's description of his homely mess, and his anecdote about the Sioux activists, both come up in the course of his riffing on what seems to be his favorite subject, which is how he doesn't particularly like children. This complaint runs through the entire story, as a sort of obsessive refrain. Indeed, Greg gives us a whole comedy routine – although he is largely serious – about how children make him feel uncomfortable; or to put it more bluntly, how "children creep me out." At one point, he tries to explain himself, defensively:

I truly don't hate children. I just don't understand them. They seem like another species. I'll help a lost child find a parent, or give a boost to a little body struggling to get a drink from a water fountain – same as I'd do for a puppy or a kitten; but I've never had the urge to be a father.

The comparison of kids to puppies and kittens is indicative; Greg is not a mean person, but I take it that he is not particularly fond of dogs or cats either. Greg is perturbed by the sheer alien *difference* of children; it seems to him that their values and desires bear no relation to his own. He doesn't "really know how to talk to kids" — or how to approach them in any other way, for that matter. With their magical beliefs – such as the fact that they "don't yet grok that delicate, all-important boundary between the animate and inanimate" – children strike him as dangerous and untrustworthy. And with their intense "single-mindedness" and their sense of "enfranchised hauteur," they make far too many absolute demands. Once they "latch on to an idea," they never let go. "Before you know it, you're arranging your whole life around their likes and dislikes."

Greg is especially upset at the way that children seem to suck up all of their parents' focus and energy. His art-school pal Babette and her husband Sunil "have looked tired, desperate and drawn for a while now," ever since they adopted their daughter Kamla. Even when Babette is cuddling Kamla, Greg says, her "eyes look sad," and her "expression ... blends frustration with concern." For her part, Babette often complains to Greg that the little girl is "making our lives hell" with her incessant clamoring and complaining. Greg laments that Babette "used to talk about gigabytes, Cronenberg and post-humanism"; but now that she is a mother, she finds it "perfectly normal to discuss [her] child's excreta with anyone who'll sit still for five minutes."

Greg's tirades about children are funny, if one-sided. He is not wrong to object to those people he calls "the righteous breeders of the flock": the ones who "spawn like frogs in springtime – or whenever the hell frogs spawn," and insist that everyone else ought to do the same. He is exasperated when friends and prospective lovers pepper him with stock questions like, "Don't you care about passing on your legacy?", and, if you don't have kids, "what are you going to do with your life, then?" Sometimes, he responds to these questions with irritated humor: "I guess I'm going to go home and put a gun to my head, since I'm clearly no use to myself or anyone else." At other times, he is breezily sarcastic about the idea that children are "supposed to be your insurance for the future; you know, to carry your name on, and shit." At still other times he says, reasonably enough, that

my life has tons of value. I just happen to think it consists of more than my genetic material ... I'm making my own legacy, thank you very much. A body of art I can point to and document.

None of this changes when Greg and Cecilia themselves become parents. It happens "by accident": when Cecilia gets pregnant despite their precautions, "we sort of dared each other to go through with it." Greg and Cecelia find themselves "curious" about "how our small brown child might change a world that desperately needs some change." For the time being, however, "baby's not about changing anyone's world but ours." In the present moment of the story, Greg and Cecilia have a two-and-a-half-year-old boy, named Russ; Greg refers to him, only half humorously, as "our creepy little alien child." Greg mentions how he and Cecilia "learned the real meaning of sleep deprivation" when the child was born; and he is now forced to acknowledge that "poo and pee are really damned important, especially when you're responsible for the life of a small, helpless being that can barely do anything else." Greg is already "freaked that" Russ has "begun making poo-poo jokes"; he absolutely doesn't want to consider that, "in a blink of an eye, barely a decade from now, [Russ'] body will be entering puberty. He'll start getting erections, having sexual thoughts." For the time being, Greg is just relieved whenever his mother is able to keep an eye on Russ, so that he can return attention to his art.

We might say that Greg is resisting what Lee Edelman denounces as *reproductive futurism*: "the pervasive invocation of the Child as the emblem of futurity's unquestioned value," and the use of this figure to consolidate the "ritual reproduction" of the normative heterosexual order. This "coercive belief in the paramount value of futurity" is central to liberal society. In the logic of reproductive futurism, everything is always and only "for the sake of future generations"; the present is systematically deprecated in favor of the future. But this exalted future never actually arrives; rather, it is interminably deferred. Whatever we do for the sake of our children, those children themselves will end up having to do for the sake of *their* children. Caught in such an endless cycle, futurity never generates anything new or different. All we do is to "reproduce the past, through displacement, in the form of the future" (Edelman 2004).

Though Greg is straight, his rejection of the mystique of childhood is not altogether different from Edelman's queer refusal of normative futurity as figured in the ideal image of the Child. When Greg says that his "legacy" is his art, rather than his "genetic material" or bloodline, he is twisting the word *legacy* (which is breeder-code for family inheritance) to refer to the present instead of the future. Greg sees his art as something that *matters*, or makes a difference, here and now, rather than as something to be left to the appreciation of future generations. Work like his – processual and site-specific, and not designed to outlast the circumstances of its installation – has little to do with the classical Western ideal of "building a monument more lasting than bronze." It is worth noting, as well, that Greg is proud of "supporting myself sort of decently" through making art. His career is an accomplishment in itself; he has no expectation of getting wealthy from it, or starting a dynasty:

I'm not a king and I'm never going to be rich. I'm not going to leave behind much wealth for someone to inherit. It's not like I'm building an empire.

My comparison of Greg's petulant complaints to Edelman's radical polemic might seem hyperbolic. But in fact, "Message in a Bottle" is literally about its narrator's confrontation with a futurity that comes to him embodied in the form of a child. Everything in the story ultimately turns upon Greg's fraught relationship with his friends' daughter Kamla. The girl is unusual, to say the least. Even at a very young age, when Babette and Sunil first adopt her, Kamla has an "outsized head" that looks "strangely adult." Indeed, "the bones in her skull are fused" already, which is something that is only supposed to happen to us "once we've stopped growing." Kamla's otherwise child-sized body is barely able to support this head, leaving her "prone to painful whiplash injuries" – not to mention that she often finds herself being ridiculed by other children as a "bobble-head." Kamla also "speaks in oddly complete sentences" for a child, saying things that are "too grown up" and too complex for her age. And it's not just her words; "something about Kamla's delivery" also "makes it easy to forget" that she's a child.

But there's more. The rest of Kamla's body, aside from her head, seems to develop very slowly. She looks far younger physically than her presumptive chronological age: "We figure she's about eight," Babette says, "but she's not much bigger than a five-year-old." Two years later, "at ten years old, people mistake her for six." Eventually, Kamla is diagnosed with Delayed Growth Syndrome (DGS), a mysterious condition shared by other children around the world who came up for adoption at the same time as she did:

It's a brand new disorder. Researchers have no clue what's causing it, or if the bodies of the kids with it will ever achieve full adulthood. Their brains, however, are way ahead of their bodies. All the kids who've tested positive for DGS are scarily smart.

Kamla seems out of phase with her time; she doesn't properly *belong* to the present moment. She is both too immature physically, and too mature mentally, for someone her ostensible age. She doesn't conform to normative expectations about child development – or indeed, to our ideas about growth and transformation more generally. Kamla's parents "send her for test after test" without learning anything new. Kamla "seems to be healthy ... Physically, anyway." But "her emotional state" remains puzzling. It is telling that Kamla cannot get along with other children her own apparent age; she gets "frustrated" and "angry" when she tries to play with them, and she complains that "I bloody hate being a kid." Even worse, she tends "to smartmouth so much at school and in our neighbourhood that it's become uncomfortable to live there anymore." Kamla and her parents are repeatedly forced to move to escape the trouble.

At one point, Greg tries to overcome his fear of children, and of Kamla in particular. He expresses the hope that,

as I watch [Kamla] grow up, I get some idea of what Russ's growing years will be like. In a way, she's his advance guard.

But he is quickly disabused of this illusion, the very next time he sees Kamla. This strange girl, with "her head wobbling as though her neck is a column of gelatin," cannot provide a model for Russ, who is "a perfect specimen; all his bits are in proportion." Greg admits to feeling "guiltily grateful that Russ, as far as we can tell, is normal." It's a bit disturbing to see Greg here retreating into an ableism – an uncritical valuing of whatever is developmentally "normal" – that he would otherwise almost certainly reject. It shows us just how unsettled he is.

We might say that Kamla fails the test, or refuses the demands, of reproductive futurism. Rather than promising to carry on her adoptive parents' "legacy," Kamla threatens to undermine it. And rather than figuring what Edelman calls "an insistence on sameness that intends to restore an Imaginary past" (*No Future*), Kamla's aberrant growth pattern – not to mention her all-around freakishness – disrupts this illusory continuity. With her perpetual anger and complaining, and her refusal or inability to fit in, Kamla seems to embody all our anxieties about difference, radical otherness, and massive social and technological change. As she herself finally puts it to Greg,

Human beings, we're becoming increasingly post-human ... Things change so quickly. Total technological upheaval of society every five to eight years. Difficult to keep up, to connect amongst the generations. By the time your Russ is a teenager, you probably won't understand his world at all.

Greg has been complaining all along that children are weirdly different from "us" (the adults). But Kamla makes him realize that he cannot expect things to return to normal, even when Russ grows up and becomes a functional adult in his own right. Such would be the resolution offered by reproductive futurism. Instead, Greg is forced to admit that what "really scares me about kids" is not the creepy reproduction of white bourgeois order, but its opposite, the threat of radical, irreversible change:

This brave new world that Cecilia and I are trying to make for our son? For the generations to follow us? We won't know how to live in it.

This is the point at which "Message in a Bottle" flips over into explicit science fiction, with its story of a future art exhibition. What

finally happens is that Kamla explains everything to Greg, by giving
him information about the future. She makes sense of all the anomalies of the story – if only Greg is willing to believe her. Science fiction
writers are often criticized for their use of *infodumps*: long expository
passages that explain the unfamiliar presuppositions of the world
of the story. Such passages are often disparaged for telling instead of
showing. Ideally, you are supposed to just drop readers into the world
of the narrative, giving them enough clues to figure out for themselves
how everything works. However, this is not always possible: you already
need some understanding of a context, in order to infer other things
about that context. Imagine a person from the European Middle Ages,
trying to make sense of electricity and fossil fuels entirely through off-
hand references and contextual clues. Infodumping is often impossible
to avoid, given that the whole point of science fiction is to present a
world that differs in significant respects from the reality that the reader
takes for granted.

Hopkinson brilliantly resolves this difficulty by making the
infodump into an event within the story – indeed, it is the story's
dramatic climax. Kamla calls Greg at three in the morning, and he
takes her for a ride and listens to her story, despite his justified fear
of encountering cops who will "think I'm some degenerate Indian
perv with a thing for little girls." Kamla has to tell him the truth,
because the story is "all over Twitter and YouTube already," and in
the tabloids as well. Instead of having the author or narrator give the
reader information about a future state, Kamla reveals the future to
Greg, and therefore indirectly to us. Since the story is set in the present, Greg is in the same position relative to what Kamla tells him, as
science fiction readers in general are relative to any text's depiction
of a future world. "Message in a Bottle" can therefore be regarded
as a meta-science-fiction story: it dramatizes the way that science
fiction as a genre is based upon the estranging irruption of futurity
into the present moment.

Kamla explains to Greg that she is in fact an art curator from the
future. She and the other "DGSers" have been sent to our present

moment – which for them is the past – in order to collect artifacts that have not survived until their own time:

Our national gallery is having a giant retrospective; tens of thousands of works of art from all over the world, and all over the world's history. They sent us back to retrieve some of the pieces that had been destroyed.

The differences between Kamla's time and our own are so great that the DGSers "have all become anthropologists here in the past, as well as curators." They find our early twenty-first century world strange, and generally feel that "your world stinks." They have trouble relating to things they regard as "ancient tech," like Greg's "video monitors." But it would seem that Kamla's era has not only more powerful technology than we do, but also a more comprehensive and enlightened understanding of culture. These future people are apparently no longer Eurocentric. They do not privilege one particular period, one particular region of the world, and one particular race and gender over all the others – as we are all too often still prone to do, even though in theory we know better. At least in this regard, Greg is on the cutting edge. Kamla somewhat condescendingly tells him that "your installation had a certain antique brio to it, Greg. Really charming." Though she also tells him that "in my world ... what you do would be obsolete."

On the other hand, some aspects of Kamla's future world seem to be very little changed from conditions that we are all too familiar with today. Kamla notes that "arts grants are hard to get in my world, too." Apparently, neoliberal economics and neoliberal governmentality are still in place several hundred years in the future. Our descendants still haven't attained a society based on abundance, instead of scarcity and austerity. This leads to reduced ambitions and diminished plans:

They wanted to send us here and back as full adults, but do you have any idea what the freight costs would have been? The insurance? ... The gallery had to scale the budget way back.

So instead of sending the arts curators themselves back in time, the future national art gallery sends clones – genetically engineered "small people ... children who [are]n't children" – to go back in their place. All the DGSers are in fact far older than they appear; Kamla, who looks like she is six, and whose adoptive parents think she is about ten, is in fact 23 years old. Not only is she a genetic clone of the curator whose interests she represents; in addition, the curator's actual memories have been "implanted" within her as well. But her chromosomes have been altered, given extra telomeres in order to "slow down aging." As a result, Kamla says, "my body won't start producing adult sex hormones for another 50 years. I won't attain my full growth till I'm in my early hundreds." She will physically bring her artifacts into the future by living through the entire span of several centuries from our time until then. It is

expensive enough to send living biomaterial back; their grant wasn't enough to pay for returning us to our time. So we're going to *grow* our way there. Those of us that survive.

"Message in a Bottle" doesn't spare us any of the grotesque and horrific consequences of this deeply compromised technological strategy. Kamla and her cohort find themselves having to spend all their time and energy in strenuous forms of pretense: "Do you know what it's like turning in schoolwork that's at a grade-five level, when we all have PhD's in our heads?" Their double consciousness on a sexual level is even worse:

The weird thing is, even though this body isn't interested in adult sex, I *remember* what it was like, remember enjoying it. It's those implanted memories from my original.

Some of the seeming-children from the future have an even harder time than Kamla does, because they get abused, just as actual children sometimes do; or they find themselves constrained as a result of "living in extremely conservative or extremely poor places"; or they fail to get adopted, and have to "make [their] own way as street kids." In any case, these people from the future have no legal rights, because in appearance they are "never old enough to be granted adult freedoms." Some of them have already died, Kamla says; and she and the rest will suffer other forms of coercive medicalized discipline: "they're probably going to institutionalise me. All of us." Such suffering, all for the sake of an art retrospective! "This fucking project better have been worth it," Kamla says.

All this is extraordinarily harsh. On first reading, it caught me entirely unawares. I had to go back and re-evaluate everything I had read up to that point. Kamla's account of time travel makes sense of all of the story's odd details – but at the price of making both Greg's discomfort with children and his pride in his art seem less innocuous and more troubling than they did previously. Unsurprisingly, Greg himself has difficulty accepting Kamla's story; after all, he does not know that he is caught in a science fiction narrative. He tries to tell himself that Kamla is "delusional ... Barmy. Loony"; or that she is "as mad as a hatter"; or that she's "been watching too many B-movies" for her own good. And yet, Greg is forced to admit that "a part of me still hopes that it's all true." It's the only resolution that he (or we) can get.

By radically revising itself with this climactic infodump, "Message in a Bottle" stages a confrontation between two different ideas about futurity. Greg is rightly irritated at the breeders who seek to replicate and perpetuate themselves in their offspring, by projecting – in the words of Jacques Derrida – "a future which is predictable, programmed, scheduled, foreseeable" (Dick and Ziering 2002). Such is the vision of what Edelman calls reproductive futurism (Edelman 2004). It is also the vision of what Mark Fisher calls *capitalist realism*: "the widespread sense that not only is capitalism the only viable political and economic system, but also that it is now impossible even to *imagine* a coherent alternative to it" (Fisher 2009).

Although their theoretical starting points are quite different, both Edelman and Fisher diagnose the ways in which contemporary neoliberal society presents itself as inevitable and unsurpassable. Neoliberal culture projects a particular idea of the future – with its calculable risk, and incessant but superficial novelty – in order to avert the possibility of any deeper disruption. Breeders investing in their kids in all the ways that irk Greg, and bankers investing in exotic financial instruments created by hedge funds, are equally involved in colonizing the future, making it commensurable with the past and present, and thereby securing it as a continuing source of profit. This is the continuing logic that leads to future art galleries scaling back their plans, and employing grotesquely unpleasant means, in order to achieve their objectives while remaining within the limits of their budget.

However, Kamla's story also opens up the prospect of another sort of future: one that is – to quote Derrida again – "totally unexpected ... totally unpredictable" (Dick and Ziering 2002). This is the future in which "things change so quickly" that we of the present moment "won't know how to live in it." Someone like Kamla, who travels back in time from such a future, might well strike us as so alien as to preclude any possibility of our being able to understand her. If the regulated, controlled-in-advance futurity of reproductive futurism and speculative finance is commonly figured in the normative form of the Child, then this *other* sort of futurity might well be figured instead as the wrong sort of offspring – or what Derrida evokes as the "birth" of a "formless, mute, infant, and terrifying form of monstrosity" (Derrida 1978).

Of course, this is Derrida's language, and not Hopkinson's. Kamla and her fellow DGSers are indeed quite disturbing, not only to Greg, but more generally to our entire society. That is why the best that these visitors from the future can hope for is to be institutionalized, and studied as medical anomalies. Still, it is only from a particularly narrow Eurocentric point of view – from the perspective of "a society," as Derrida is careful to say, "from which I do not exclude myself" (Derrida 1978) – that any such difference must be seen as formless monstrosity, or that the only alternative to a programmed and normative future is the absolute negativity of "no future." The stark alternative we find in Derrida and Edelman is something like the philosophical equivalent of H. P. Lovecraft's cosmology, in which a flimsy veneer of white European order is our only bulwark against the chaotic horror of the inhuman Elder Gods. This makes for a woefully impoverished choice – even if it is to the credit of Derrida and Edelman that, as opposed to Lovecraft, they are more than willing to side with Dagon and Cthulhu.

But "Message in a Bottle" suggests – as do many other works of Afrofuturism, not to mention Indigenous, queer, and other futurisms – that Derrida's monstrous deconstruction of order, and Edelman's "radical challenge to the very value of the social itself," are not the only frameworks in which to conceive of alternative futurities. Kamla tells Greg that he would find her future world almost as oppressive and unpleasant as she finds his (and our) present one; but she still tries to assure him that, although "ours is a society that you would probably find strange," nonetheless "we do have moral codes." She warns Greg that politics and social values, no less than technologies, will be radically different in the future from what they are now; but "art helps us know how to do change." This is why she is a curator, and why she was "excited by the idea, the crazy, wonderful idea" of going back in time to recover lost works of art – despite all the difficulties and dangers involved.

Greg tries to get a modicum of comfort from this by thinking that at least Kamla is interested in his art. Indeed, he is vain enough that his "heart's performing a tympanum of joy" at the very suggestion that "The Excavations" might appear in a distant-future art retrospective. In spite of everything, Greg is still excited by the thought that his "legacy" might "get to go the future" after all.

But alas, this is not to be. Greg's hope turns out to be yet another misconception. In one final twist of irony, Kamla tells Greg that she isn't interested in his installation itself. Rather, she has come back in time to recover a seashell that she finds buried in the dirt covering the floor of the gallery. Greg himself can "barely remember putting that in there"; it is one of the "blanks that trigger no stories." The shell is only part of the exhibition by chance, because "the dig where I got it from used to be underwater a few centuries ago." Greg has no idea that, in the future, this seashell will be regarded as a greater work of art than

anything he or his contemporaries have made. As Kamla explains
to him,

Human beings aren't the only ones who make art ... Every shell is a life
journal ... made out of the very substance of its creator, and left as a record
of what it thought, even if we can't understand exactly what it thought ... Of
its kind, the mollusc that made this shell is a genius. The unique conform-
ation of the whorls of its shell expresses a set of concepts that haven't been
explored before by the other artists of its species. After this one, all the others
will draw on and riff off its expression of its world. They're the derivatives, but
this is the original.

Greg finds this difficult to accept. It is "familiar territory" for him
to concede that "bower birds make pretty nests to attract a mate.
Cetaceans sing to each other." But he still insists on human exception-
alism: "we're the only ones who make art *mean*; who make it comment
on our everyday reality." Kamla, however, denies this. Other animals
also have values, express meanings, and comment upon the realities
they encounter. The poignancy of this claim for a nonhuman aesthetics
rests upon a new, expanded understanding of the limits of communication. We need to respect the artistic creations of other entities, Kamla
says, even though

we don't always know what they're saying, we can't always know the reality
on which they're commenting. Who knows what a sea cucumber thinks of the
conditions of its particular stretch of ocean floor? ... Sometimes interpretation
is a trap. Sometimes we need to simply observe.

This is not inconsistent with the mainstream of modern (post-
Kantian) Western aesthetics. Kant poses a paradox at the heart of what
he calls "aesthetic taste." On the one hand, each instance of beauty
that we encounter is unique; it is irreducible to, and incommensurable with, any other. On the other hand, and at the very same time,
my ability to find something beautiful implies a certain "universal

communicability": that is to say, my encounter with an instance of beauty is not a private, inner experience, but something that I can point out and describe, and share with others (Kant 2000). In other words, we can *recognize* the beauty and power of an aesthetic expression, even though "we don't always know what they're saying, we can't always know the reality on which they're commenting." Aesthetic experience allows us to approach points of view that aren't our own, and that are strange to us; we can appreciate these other perspectives, even though we cannot adopt them, or even fully understand them. Such is the basis of Kamla's work as a curator (or perhaps we should say, of the work of her "original," Vanda, whose memories as well as genes she shares).

The real question for Western aesthetics is how far this process of recognition – even in the absence of comprehension – extends. Up through the mid-twentieth century, the circle was fairly small: recognition was only accorded to a small number of elite European and North American works, usually created by white men. Over the past half century, the circle has greatly expanded. This is due to two developments: first, the increased recognition of works by white women and by people of color; and second, the breakdown of the once rigid boundary between "high" and "mass" culture.

"Message in a Bottle" suggests that aesthetic recognition will continue to widen in the years to come. Kamla explains to Greg how "the nascent identity politics as expressed by artists of the twentieth and twenty-first centuries," such as Greg himself, "was the progenitor of current speciesism." This latter term seems to designate the "defining concept through which we understand what it means to be human animals," by grasping the parallels, as well as the differences, between our own aesthetic expressions and those of other organisms. The expansion of our own ability to recognize the "universal communicability" of the works of many cultures, not just the white European one, leads ultimately to a still broader recognition of aesthetic works and processes across the species barrier.

What are we to make of this extension? Addie Hopes, commenting on another text by Hopkinson (her 2007 novel *The New Moon's Arms*), points to a tension between Black Studies and what has come to be known as the "nonhuman turn" in the humanities (cf. Grusin):

Black studies scholars have long been suspicious of (white) scholars' attempts to break down the lines between human and the nonhuman, particularly as black *humanity* has only recently begun to be seen as such within the academy and is still, politically, a fight far from won.

(Hopes 2018)

But Hopes notes how Hopkinson conciliates this opposition with her mythical invention of the "sea people" (or "black mermaids") in *The New Moon's Arms*. These people are the descendants of kidnapped Africans who escaped the Middle Passage by jumping off slave ships and adapting to life in the ocean. They are web-fingered, and they have the power to transform themselves at will into seals. In this way, the sea people both assert their humanity against a racist system that denied it to them, *and* cross the species barrier that would estrange human beings from all other forms of life. Hopes reads this double movement in terms of Sylvia Wynter's notion of *genres of the human*:

Hopkinson's mermaid maroons inspire readers to do as Katherine McKittrick asks us to do: to "recognize 'human genres' other than those of Man ... and open up the possibility for ... imagining alternative forms of being" ... and becoming-with: intimate and co-constitutive relations between humans, monk seals, gods, red snapper fish, and toxic pollutants ...

(Hopes 2018, citing McKittrick and Wynter 2016)

Here, recognizing other genres of humanity is continuous with recognizing nonhumans as well, and establishing "intimate and co-constitutive relations" with them. The crucial move is to reject the hegemony of capital-M "Man," which is an exclusionary, white European concept. An opening to other genres of the human is *also* an opening to many sorts of nonhumans, and to futures (in the plural) outside the purview of capitalist realism and reproductive futurism.

"Message in a Bottle" also offers us such a prospect: a future that exceeds the boundaries of our conventionally humanist understanding, and that may thereby allow for hopeful developments that we are not currently able to imagine. Instead of bringing Greg's artistic "legacy" into a future that would just be another expanded repetition of the past and the present, Kamla charges Greg with the responsibility for nurturing a different future, an odd future, one that he does not and cannot ever experience for himself. Kamla is all too oppressively aware of the horrors – institutionalization or worse – that our current society has in store for her. She is still a small person, without the rights and powers of an adult, regardless of what is in her head. She knows that it won't be forever; as she defiantly says, "we're going to outlive all our captors." But she also knows that she is in for a lot of grief along the way. At the very end of the story, she begs Greg to keep the seashell safe for her in the meantime. "It's your ticket to the future," she tells him. Greg for his part resents this. He ends the story with a zinger: "I lied. I fucking hate kids." But I am inclined to think that he remains bound, nonetheless, by Kamla's charge to him – or, to put it differently, by the promise he did not give.

Chapter 6

Dark Eden

Chris Beckett's 2012 novel *Dark Eden* (Beckett 2012) – together with its sequels, *Mother of Eden* (Beckett 2015) and *Daughter of Eden* (Beckett 2016) – tells the story of a small group of human beings stranded, far from Earth, on a dark rogue planet, somewhat ironically named Eden. This planet is alone in the cosmos. It does not circle any star, and it does not have any moons. This means that it is perpetually dark. There are no seasons, and no diurnal cycles. As Eden lacks a sun, its sole energy source is geothermal. Heat arises from deep within the planet's core, and warms the surface to Earth-like temperatures. The gravity, too, seems to be Earth-normal; and the planet has plenty of water, and an Earth-like atmosphere that is thick enough to preserve the heat. The lower altitudes of the planet's surface are warm and fertile; while the higher elevations are cold enough to be covered in ice and snow. The skies are usually overcast; but sometimes the clouds congeal into fog and warm rain (at the lower elevations) or snow (at the higher ones). At other times, the ubiquitous clouds dissipate for a brief while; the air gets cooler, and in the blackness of the sky the inhabitants can see what they call the "Starry Swirl." Apparently this is our own galaxy, the Milky Way, appearing in its full spiraling glory.

Living organisms have evolved in this environment, both on land and in water, in forms roughly analogous to what we know as plants and animals. Of course, Eden's plant-analogues – which the inhabitants call trees and flowers – do not photosynthesize as Earth plants do. Rather, they use the planet's geothermal energy for fuel, pumping it up from deep beneath the surface. They "warm the air with their trunks," and drive the ecosystem of the planet as a whole. Animals, for their part, bask in this warmth; they either forage upon the plants directly, or prey

upon other animals. These animals are roughly analogous to terrestrial organisms – the inhabitants call them bats, monkeys, leopards,
and so on – but they are unrelated to Earth life, and alien to human
sensibilities and expectations. They have "green-black blood and two
hearts and six limbs," together with "round and flat" eyes that "don't
turn from side to side" the way that our eyes do. They don't have facial
expressions or bodily gestures that we know how to interpret. People
find it hard to empathize with them.

The native life-forms provide Eden with its only light. The plants
display softly glowing "lanternflowers"; animals similarly have "soft
white lanterns on the tops of their heads." The forests and valleys of
Eden are thereby illuminated with "a dim light – pink, white, blue and
yellow." Such light "wasn't much brighter than moonlight is on Earth";
but it is enough to allow the human inhabitants to see. However, the
fertile areas, lit by abundant plant and animal life, are separated from
one another by "Snowy Dark" – much more sparsely populated snowy
ridges and mountain ranges. At these higher elevations, everything is
"dark dark" and "*cold* cold."

How did human beings come to inhabit Eden? It was all an accident. Five astronauts from Earth came upon the planet after passing
through a wormhole. Three of them had illicitly commandeered a
spaceship in order to go on a joyride; the other two were orbital police,
who followed and tried to stop them. They all ended up landing on
Eden after damaging their spaceship. Two of the astronauts – Angela
Young, one of the cops, and Tommy Schneider, one of the joyriders –
remained on the surface. The other three left, hoping to signal Earth
for help; Angela and Tommy never saw them again. *Dark Eden* takes
place some 160 years after this first landing. All the human inhabitants
of the planet are descended from the founding heterosexual couple
who remained. Tommy was a Jewish man from Brooklyn; Angela was
a Black woman from London. We are told that they were not exactly
companions by choice:

They say that Angela and Tommy didn't get on so well. It's said he got angry
when he didn't get his way. It's said she was full of bitterness for what he'd done

to her … She'd never have come here at all of her own choice, and she'd never have been with a man like him either.

Nonetheless, as the sole human beings on the planet, Tommy and Angela felt impelled to be fruitful and multiply. They had a son and three daughters, who in turn had more children, and so on. One of the results of this inbreeding, or lack of genetic diversity, is an accumulation of birth defects: many of Angela and Tommy's descendants are "batfaces" (people with cleft lips and palates) or "clawfeet" (people with clubfeet). A smaller number are intellectually disabled.

At the time *Dark Eden* begins, there are slightly over five hundred human inhabitants of Eden. They are all huddled together in Circle Valley, an enclave bounded by mountains and cliffs on all sides. The people think of themselves as a single (capital-F) Family, subdivided into eight "groups" or tribes, each of which has its own last name. The people of Eden are hunter-gatherers, who eke out their existence at a subsistence level. They live in a state of what might be considered primitive communism. They all work together, and equally share their food and other goods. Everyday life rests mostly upon the guidance of custom and myth. There are few explicit laws, and most decisions are made by consensus. Authority, such as it is, resides in the hands of the elders, and particularly the women. "Having a slip" – the term the people on Eden use for having sex – is a frequent and quite casual activity. The only rules about it are that "you mustn't slip with a child or with anyone that doesn't want to do it … and grown men mustn't slip with young girls." There is no monogamy, no sense of anything like a nuclear family, and no "ownership" of wives by husbands. Children are raised collectively; they retain ties with their mothers and their maternal siblings and cousins, but most of the time they do not know who their fathers are.

Despite all this, the people of Eden do not think of themselves as living in a paradise. Rather, they acutely feel that they live diminished lives, compared to their ancestors on Earth. This primitive Eden is already a fallen one. The people have heard stories about – and bemoan the lack of – such seemingly magical things as "Rayed Yo" (*radio*), "Telly vision" (*television*), and "Computer," not to mention, more generally, "metal and plastic" and "lecky-trickity" (*electricity*). As the altered words suggest, their language has also been stripped down and simplified. It's hard to retain the integrity of words whose referents and concepts are entirely unavailable. Some of Edenic speech also sounds a bit like baby talk. For instance, the people use repeated adjectives instead of intensifiers: they say "dark dark" instead of "very dark." Everything on Eden, from language to lifestyle, is something of a degraded replica. Everything is haunted by the ghosts of what is missing.

Above all, the people of Eden are aware of being deprived of their "far-off world full of light ... Our eyes need the bright light." Their legends tell them that the Sun of Earth is "so bright that it would burn out your eyes if you stared at it." But they have no way to imagine what such illumination would actually be like; it goes too far beyond the bounds of their actual experience. Instead, they associate bright light with promises of salvation. They see themselves as exiles, and desperately want to return to the place of their origins:

We live as if Eden wasn't where we really lived at all but just a camp like hunters make when they stay out in forest for a few wakings. We're only waiting here to go back to where we really belong ... We shouldn't *be* here, that's the real problem: it wasn't the world we were made for. We were meant to live in light ... We were trapped inside a dark little cave with no way out of it. And even though I'd never known anything else, and probably never *would* do. I longed and longed for that different world that was full of light.

This almost Gnostic yearning is the core of what can only be called the Edenites' religion. The people live in hope for the moment when – however long it takes – a spaceship arrives from Earth, in order to take them back to their true home. Perhaps the spaceship will also take back the bones of the dead, and restore them to life. Other religious motifs stand out as well. For instance, the people tell the story of the astronaut Michael, who – just like Adam in the Bible – first "named the animals and plants." This explains why the alien life-forms of Eden have Earth-reminiscent names.

By the start of *Dark Eden*, however, the ostensibly temporary condition of exile has already lasted for six generations. The Polish aphorist Stanislaw Lec wrote that gossip grown old becomes myth; and Chris Beckett himself has noted that "a lot of the Old Testament is small domestic stories elevated to a mythical level" (Goldschlager 2014). We literally see this process take place in Eden. The whole society is organized around the ostensibly "True Story" of Angela and Tommy. The Story contains many unpleasant details. We hear about Angela's outbursts of rage, and her despair after losing the ring that her parents had given her back on Earth; Tommy's violence ("once twice he even hit her"), and his ultimate suicide; and the brother-sister and father-daughter incest that were needed for the Family to grow in its early days. But this old gossip, however changed over years of oral transmission, is the only tradition or heritage that the people of Eden have.

Gossip still remains the basis of sociality on Eden, even in the present time of the novel. Several of the book's "newhair" (*teenaged* or *adolescent*) narrators complain about it at length:

You can't do anything in Family without everyone knowing about it, and weighing it up, and picking it over, and making their bloody minds up about what they thought about it ... every bloody little thing that happened, in no time everyone in Family was talking talking about it and poring over it and prodding it and poking at it and clucking their tongues over it ... In fact, we were so on top of one another, so in each others' lives and in each others' heads, we were hardly separate from one another at all ... it made me feel like I couldn't breathe.

This suffocating intimacy is only reinforced when the whole Family gathers, every "Any Virsry" (*anniversary*), to perform the rituals that bind them together. They retell the gossip-turned-myth of the True Story. The Oldest, victims of dementia, and propped against a wall "like three empty skin bags," drone on about the early days of the colony. "Mementoes" (i.e. relics, objects that once belonged to Angela and Tommy: "the Boots, the Belt, the Backpack, the Kee Board") and "Models" (i.e. replicas, chintzy little toy models of spaceships and airplanes and cars and houses) are passed around for inspection.

One of the tribes does a "Show," a dramatic reenactment of the saga of Angela and Tommy. As the ceremony goes on, the older people are relieved and reassured, the children are entertained, but the newhairs are alienated and "bored." The stasis of tradition, or of gossip-turned-myth, can only do so much.

Dark Eden actually starts at the point of a looming social crisis, although this only becomes apparent gradually. The material cause is environmental stress. The Family lives in one small valley, closed off from the rest of the planet by dark, icy mountains. As their numbers expand, the people find themselves overexploiting and depleting their limited resources. Animals become scarcer and harder to catch; people are forced to adopt food sources they previously disdained. Tradition doesn't offer any suggestion for dealing with the crisis, aside from working harder and eating less. Family can only fumble about, as it is

full of stupid people, full of hateful, disappointed people, full of sour people, full of ignorant people who never thought anything through for themselves.

The end of abundance means, however, that something has to change. The combination of scarcity with adolescent boredom and restlessness, not to mention male aggression no longer held in check, makes for an explosive mix. The novel is mostly concerned with how the established society of Eden breaks down, and what replaces it. *Dark Eden* therefore provides the narrative of what in other language might be called the Fall of humanity – albeit this is a secularized and material-istic Fall, driven by ecological limits rather than by original sin.

There is a complex irony to this account. For, as we have already seen, the society of Eden, at the start of the novel, is already a fallen one. It defines itself largely in terms of exile and deprivation, and yearns for a supposed lost plenitude. And yet, this minor, diminished society is still a sort of paradise, from which the people suffer yet another Fall. In the course of the book, we descend from gossip-turned-myth into history, from harmony and stasis into rupture and betrayal, and from peaceful, egalitarian matriarchal communism into patriarchy, private property, and militaristic violence.

The storytelling of *Dark Eden* is divided among eight first-person narrators. As the unity of Edenic society is shattered, we cannot understand what is going on from a single point of view. The various narrators both embody, and focus, the tensions beneath the surface of Family life. Most of them are newhairs, but they also include the querulous Mitch London, one of the Oldest, and Caroline Brooklyn, the official Family Head, the closest thing to a leader that the old society has. The divergences among these narrators work to convey the way that Eden's small society splinters in the course of the novel. One index of this general collapse – much more a symptom than a cause – is the end of common assent to the Family's mythical narrative. People stop believing in the value, here and now, of a communal life; some of them also stop believing in the promise of an ultimate salvific return to Earth. At the end of the novel, the people even discover the crashed vehicle in which the three missing astronauts tried to call for help. It is evident that they died without ever having a chance to do so. This destroys the people's hope, but it is also a potential source of renewal, or secular rededication: "now we know for sure we can just get on with things and don't have to wait around for Earth."

John Redlantern is the most important of the book's narrators, and the character who is most instrumental in changing Edenic society. John is a restless newhair; he perceives the danger of limited and decreasing resources, and he feels stifled by the Family's conservative adherence to tradition. First he disrupts Any Virsry with his impertinent questions; then he coolly and deliberately desecrates the Family's central symbols. As a result, the Family sends him into exile – something that has never happened on Eden before. When John leaves, he is joined by a few other newhairs, who in effect become his acolytes. This sort of hierarchy between a single leader and a mass of followers is something else that has never been seen on Eden before. John's followers are united, at least, in the hope that his vision will make it possible for them to establish a new social order elsewhere.

The exodus of John and his followers requires – and indeed leads to – an energetic burst of social and technological innovation. There isn't enough room for them in Circle Valley; aside from the limited resources, they are still too close for comfort to the Family. John wants to cross the dark, snowy mountains – something that tradition opposes, and that nobody has ever thought to do before. But in order to accomplish this, John and his followers must devise new means of transportation, domesticate some of the native fauna, and produce warm clothing for the first time. By the end of the novel, John and his group have succeeded in all of these tasks; on the other side of the mountains they find a new fertile region, one that is far larger, and richer in resources, than Circle Valley.

John Redlantern might well be the unproblematic hero of a more traditional science fiction novel. And indeed, in her review of *Dark Eden*, N. K. Jemisin accuses Chris Beckett precisely of this:

What really dims Eden's glow, however, is the 1950s ethos underpinning the whole thing ... John himself is that most threadbare of science fiction types: the impossibly handsome, impossibly forward-thinking young man who gets the prettiest girl with no particular effort, and saves the day through sheer bloody-mindedness.

(Jemisin 2014)

I think, however, that this is an ungenerous, and unfairly reductive, view of the novel. For Beckett gives us a far more nuanced and – dare I say? – *dialectical* view of John Redlantern, and the changes he initiates, than Jemisin implies. Social tensions (or what traditional Marxists call *contradictions*) may well impel or necessitate change, but this does not mean that the change is automatically progressive or good. It is true that John is genuinely imaginative; he is able to see problems before other people become aware of them, and to envision alternatives that wouldn't cross anyone else's mind. However, although John knows that things have to change, he only wants – and he will only accept – change on his own particular terms. He hates when somebody else takes the initiative. As the Family Head Caroline Brooklyn tells us, what John's disruption "was really about was him being the hero of the story, and no one else." Or as John's first supporter and sometime companion Tina Spiketree puts it, John "can't leave a thing alone, he can't bear anything that hasn't got his personal mark on it."

John has something of a messianic obsession. No matter what happens, he requires his followers "to go on believing in me," and not listen to anyone else. He is always calculating the angles and looking for a tactical advantage. When his friends first come to join him in exile, for instance, he doesn't go out to greet them, but hides instead, because "it needed to be *them* coming to *me*, not me going to them. I didn't want to have to owe them anything, not when I had so many plans." And later, when the group runs into difficulties that he cannot solve, and his cousin Jeff Redlantern works things out instead, John regards his cousin's success as "yet another problem that I had to figure out how to fix."

In order to maintain his authority, John never tells anyone what he really feels and thinks. He always keeps his face "still still like a mask." He continually monitors and manipulates the image he projects to others. He knows on some level that he needs collaborators, and that he cannot accomplish anything alone. But as Tina notes, he is "scared" of her, or of anyone else whom he might have to treat as an "equal" instead of a follower or a hanger-on. Tina joins John's group, in preference to staying with Family. But she is continually annoyed that John had "expected us to follow him and trust him, but he hadn't trusted any of *us* at all." Indeed, John doesn't even seem capable of respecting others or treating them with any degree of reciprocity. Jeff complains to John at one point that he is acting as if "everything in the world is just stuff for you to use for your plans." And Tina says that John "just didn't quite get it. He didn't quite get that other people apart from him had their own thoughts and their own plans and their own things in their heads."

Moreover, since John's talent consists in "breaking out of something old and making something new," he is only satisfied when he is shaking things up. He is "happy happy happy" even or especially when he has "bad bad news ... he liked having trouble to deal with." On the other hand, John is unable to accept situations in which people are actually settled and contented. As Tina puts it, "ordinary waking-by-waking stuff seemed to make him restless and uneasy: the chit-chat, the joking about, the little arguments, the kids, the chores." When John's group finally reaches a situation of sufficient abundance so that "you didn't need to have everyone working working all waking long just to get enough to eat," all John can do is fret and brood and complain. He scorns his own friends and followers as people who

just try and make things easy and comfortable right now ... if I left it to the others, no plans would get made. They'd just eat and sleep and play and slip, until something happened to stop them.

In other words, John is somebody who doesn't want to live, under any circumstances, in a peaceful, egalitarian, and unfallen condition. He scorns the very idea that things could be "easy and comfortable." Even if Eden had not already been in a state of crisis, he would have sought to provoke one – although, without the objective existence of economic stress, he probably would not have succeeded. John compulsively needs to break things, if only so that he can be the one to fix them. In showing us this, *Dark Eden* offers a critique, rather than an endorsement, of the "1950s ethos" of golden-age science fiction about which Jemisin complains.

John's opposite number, and his biggest enemy, is his somewhat older kinsman David Redlantern. David is by far the nastiest character in the book, and the closest the novel gets to a traditional antagonist. He is not one of the eight narrators, and we only see him through others' eyes. From the very beginning, David is highly unpleasant, with his "angry spluttery voice," his aggressive sarcasm, and his inclination toward violence. He always has it in for John, in particular. David is one of those angry men who "want the story to be all about *them*," and who "turn into bullies and try and control people." He is "cruel and cold and hard," a "sour sarcastic lump of misery," and nobody likes him – but many people fear him, even at the start of the book, when Eden is entirely peaceful.

Questions of disability have their place here as well. (Chris Beckett, a former social worker, is sensitive to issues of disability and ableism.) Some people in the Family say that David is the way he is because he is a batface: he is embittered because he is ugly, and because he has always been "left on the outside of things." Ableism is certainly a problem in Edenic society; as the batface Sue Redlantern (John's aunt and Jeff's mother) remarks, "we batfaces took a lot of stick and we had to stand up for each other." Nevertheless, it is worth noting that other batfaces, especially the women, are generally described as "kind and giving," or "always cheerful cheerful," or "as sweet-natured as anyone could be." David's anger cannot be blamed on his disability; he exhibits a distinctively masculine pathology, though it is initially kept in check by Eden's matriarchy.

David Redlantern is the very first to take offense at John's transgressions; and he is louder about his objections than anyone else. But David's ostensible defense of tradition is just as destructive of the old order as John's innovations are, if not more so. When John desecrates and destroys the Family's central symbols, David immediately demands that he be put to death: "Hang him up from a spiketree like we hang a buckskin out to dry ... Spike him up to burn, like Hitler did to Jesus." (The name "Hitler" is known in Eden's lore as the murderer of "the Juice" – i.e. *the Jews* – and their leader Jesus; this combination of the Holocaust and the Crucifixion, neither of which is really understood by anyone on Eden, is another example of how the Family's oral tradition works.)

David, like John, is quick to recruit followers and flunkies – and especially disaffected newhairs – to his cause. Soon he has formed an (all-male) order of Guards, with himself as the Head of Guards. The Guards are "thirty forty young men, [who] grinned and smirked at each other with their big blackglass spears over their shoulders." They intimidate everyone else, and arrogate special privileges for themselves. Caroline Brooklyn and the older women are stripped of authority; they are simply ignored by David and the Guards, and eased out of the picture. Everyone else is intimidated into obeying the Guards' instructions. Almost without anyone's concrete awareness of what is going on, the Family is transformed from a peaceful, egalitarian matriarchy into a violent, militaristic, and hierarchical patriarchy.

The last time we see the formerly peaceful people of Circle Valley, they have become a lynch mob, vowing vengeance against John and his followers, all of them chanting: "*Kill! Kill! Kill! Kill! Kill! Kill!*" Events outpace deliberative awareness. Many of the people, and even some of the Guards, are still a bit "troubled by what was happening." But as Sue Redlantern tells us, "it made no difference, though." If members of the Guard "didn't do what they were told, they were at risk themselves." In other words, David's militaristic coup has a self-reinforcing dynamic. People are impelled to join in, because other people have already joined in. If I don't want to get in trouble by showing my doubts and hesitation, I had better prove my loyalty by persecuting anyone else who dares to express their doubts.

The clash between John's and David's factions leads, inexorably, to the (re)invention of rape and murder: practices that are all too familiar to us on Earth, but that were previously unknown on Eden. Even though a truce between the two groups is ostensibly in place, some of David's followers go out to stir up trouble. They beat and very nearly kill Jeff, and they are on the verge of raping Tina. But John and some of his other male followers come to the rescue; in their turn, they kill the three aggressors. Having committed the first murders on Eden, John and his associates have evidently (as Tina puts it)

changed. They'd changed completely. They were trembling worse than me, they were shaking all over, and their faces were all blotchy and twisted and puffed up, so you couldn't tell if they were scared or angry or excited or ashamed or what.

There is no going back from a change like this. And although John and his friends did in fact act in self-defense, this is not really an alibi. Murder and rape are no longer unthinkable; they are now real possibilities in Eden. And John and his people are just as capable of these deeds as David and his people are. Once again, there is an obvious Biblical parallel: the story of Cain and Abel. But in *Dark Eden*'s secularized version of the Fall, the first murder is not a consequence of eating the apple and being expelled from the Garden; rather, it is the precipitating and irreversible moment of the Fall itself.

Dark Eden, however – in this matter quite unlike the Bible – insists that the state of a given society's gender relations, in addition to being of concern in itself, is also an index, and a harbinger, of social relations more generally. Tina Spiketree, despite being one of John's first supporters, is presciently aware of what his innovations will do to gender relations. "The time of men was coming," she reflects; "in this new, broken-up world it would be the men that would get ahead." Women will not only be subordinated under David's rule, but under John's as well. Having sex will no longer be entirely consensual on both sides; "a time was coming," Tina reflects, when a man would be able to "do to me *whatever* he pleased and whenever he felt like it, with which-ever bit of my body he chose."

Tina's grim premonitions are correct; and they apply to John's group, as much as they do to David's. When John sets up his new society, he becomes obsessed with enforcing monogamy, so that a man "knows which kids he was the dad of." John also pays no attention to child-rearing, which he regards as women's work – except when he is assured that the child in question is biologically his own. John and Tina are sort of a couple, and he doesn't want her to have sex with anybody else. Tina is strong and independent enough to reject John's demands; but it is unlikely that her children and her grandchildren will have a similar freedom. John also tries to hide from Tina the fact that he him-self is doing precisely what he wants to stop her from doing: having sex on the side with other people. The double standard, and the sexual div-ision of labor, go together with John's overall drive to put his stamp on everything, and to reform Edenic society in his own image.

John's group and David's group are finally not all that different from one another; their very antagonism ties them together. John puts aside his disturbed feelings after the first killings, and convinces him-self that they were justified for reasons of policy; he see this as the best way to manage his group efficiently. David more simply just revels self-righteously in the call to murder, since this helps him push for-ward his own project of domination. John's people continue to be the innovators, but David's people quickly imitate and adopt all of their inventions. David and his men are overt rapists, in a way that John and his followers are not (or at least not yet); but we can see the same ten-dencies of male domination at work on both sides.

By the second and third volumes of Beckett's trilogy, taking place two centuries after *Dark Eden*, the "Johnfolk" and the "Davidfolk" have divided most of the known world between them. The two societies are enemies, and they come to war. But both societies are male-dominated and extremely hierarchical, with privileged ruling groups, militias to enforce order, and the vast majority of the people forced into incessant and difficult labor. We can only conclude that John's stress on innovation, and David's stress on tradition, are in fact two sides of the same coin. They are both ultimately grounded in resentment: John resents what he sees as the Family's oppressive traditions, and David resents what he sees as the undue independence of young people and of women. They both channel discontent into urges for expansion, in contrast to the steady state of the earlier Family. And they both undermine communal solidarity, by subordinating it to the commands of an individual masculine will.

In tracing these developments, the *Eden* trilogy might well be described as a work of *speculative anthropology*. Beckett offers us an updated, and highly self-reflexive, version of the sort of nineteenth-century ethnographic speculation that we find in books like Johann Jakob Bachofen's *Mother-Right* (1861), Lewis Henry Morgan's *Ancient Society* (1877), and above all Friedrich Engels' *The Origin of the Family, Private Property, and the State* (1884). These works all tell the story of a primordial matriarchal and egalitarian communism, and of a secular Fall from this state into one of patriarchy and wide class divisions.

These nineteenth-century works were largely deprecated in the twentieth century, on the grounds that they make overly broad generalizations on the basis of piecemeal empirical evidence. But it is worth noting that, despite all the discoveries and research advances of the past century, our evidence on human origins and human evolution is *still* unavoidably piecemeal, and likely to remain so. The question of human social and cultural development *requires* speculation of one sort or another, since there is too much that can never be objectively traced and reconstructed. In social history, no less than in evolutionary biology, we cannot get anywhere without organizing our data into narratives; and these narratives must involve some sort of speculation, since the information upon which they are based is necessarily incomplete.

However, not all forms of narrative speculation are equal. Consider, for instance, the discipline of so-called "evolutionary psychology." It claims that universal "human nature" is genetically determined and socially invariant, and that it consists of instincts and traits that evolved in primordial human populations over the course of the Pleistocene, and have been unchanged since (Barkow et al. 1995). Evolutionary psychology's flat denial of sociocultural influences and differences coincides with its tendency to read our present circumstances and assumptions back into all of evolutionary history. Thus it uncritically adopts, and projects all the way back into the Pleistocene, both a "1950s ethos" with regard to gender norms, and a distinctly neoliberal conception of *Homo economicus* (according to which atomistic individuals compete in zero-sum games for relative advantage).

The evidence for the story told by evolutionary psychology remains exceedingly slender and dubious (see, e.g., the critiques by Kitcher 1985 and by Richardson 2007). And its assumptions are overly narrow and reductionistic; for instance, it has no room for an evolutionary approach that includes feedback from cultural development (such as that of Tomlinson 2018). But perhaps we should be wary of simply denouncing evolutionary psychology for its "just-so stories," as so many of its opponents, from Stephen Jay Gould onward, have done (Gottlieb 2012). The problem is not that evolutionary psychology resorts to storytelling *per se*, but rather that its stories are so lame and simplistic. These stories tend to isolate individual traits from their broader contexts, and give univocal explanations for these traits. Such explanations always come down to saying that a particular trait gives the organism that inherits it a particular adaptive advantage; but no consideration is given to how the various adaptations interact with and feed back upon one another, or how they alter and feed back upon the very environments to which they are supposed to adapt. These stories also fail to come to grips with the way that they themselves work *as stories*; they pretend to be more objective, more generalizable, and more empirically grounded, than they actually are. Evolutionary psychology is particularly poor at coming to grips with aesthetics. This is a serious problem, since aesthetic considerations are deeply embedded both in the act of telling stories, and in the life situations to which these stories refer.

In contrast, science fiction writers like Chris Beckett, and the nineteenth-century speculative anthropologists upon whom he implicitly draws, tell far better and richer stories than the evolutionary psychologists do. Engels relied upon the best anthropology of his own day, much of which is now obsolete; but he was closely attentive to the complex interactions between social and economic conditions and gender relations. In general, the narratives of speculative anthropology are far more sophisticated and incisive, and far more aware of multiple, overlapping and interacting, causes, than are those of evolutionary psychology. Where evolutionary psychology sees our contemporary gender stereotypes and economic traits as having existed for all of human history as a result of narrowly adaptive mechanisms, speculative anthropology rather seeks to envision the *particular historical and social conditions* that could have led to the emergence of particular stereotypes and traits.

Of course, *Dark Eden* differs from the texts of Bachofen, Morgan, and Engels, in that it is *overtly* a work of science fiction. I consider this an advantage. Beckett's account of social transformation, unlike these earlier ones, has the virtue of being explicitly and self-consciously an act of fabulation. Of course, Beckett tries to make his speculations as plausible and far-reaching as possible; but he does not claim that they tell us, once and for all, who and what we really (deeply and truly) are. Rather, *Dark Eden* presents itself as a heuristic parable. The novel offers us a speculative reconstruction of human origins; but it calls attention to this very act of reconstruction as a narrative fabulation in its own right.

This is why the novel's speculative storytelling includes so much reflection on storytelling itself. When Angela and Tommy are first stranded on Eden, they are faced with the task of rebuilding human civilization from scratch. But they do not do this in a vacuum; like Robinson Crusoe, they have a legacy from the past. Karl Marx sarcastically notes that Robinson Crusoe starts out, not only with all the stuff that he is salvages from the shipwreck, but also with his already-ingrained bourgeois values and assumptions. Even as he builds himself a shelter, and makes his own garments and tools, so also he "soon begins, like a good Englishman, to keep a set of books" (Marx 1976). Angela and Tommy similarly rely, at the very least, upon their memories of life on Earth, or what might be called their intellectual capital. Even six generations later, the people of Eden are still dominated by the narratives that have thus been handed down to them.

Later in the novel, even as John Redlantern disrupts the Family, he is acutely aware that his own actions are themselves already the elements of a new narrative:

It wasn't just in the *future* that this meeting would become a story to be acted out. Even now, even when it was happening for the first time round, it had already become a story in a way, with me as an actor in it, playing a part, and not just being myself. *I* was acting me.

Of course, this goes along with how John shapes himself as an agent, manipulating his own image, and holding back from revealing his inner thoughts to others. We might well say that John, unlike everyone else before him in Eden, is conscious of being a historical figure. This self-consciousness is the reason why his actions move the story of Eden out of the realm of myth, and into that of history. John is aware of his present actions as part of a story-in-process, because he realizes that his actions have the power to determine the future, by moving it onto a new path. But John also discovers that the story in which he sees himself as an actor is not entirely his to control:

It had never occurred to me before that the story of John Redlantern might end up as the story of a famous killer, the first one in Eden ever to do for another human being. But now that story suddenly took shape in my mind.

John cannot entirely shape the future, because he cannot eliminate unplanned circumstances and unintended outcomes from his story. As Marx famously wrote, human beings "make their own history, but they do not make it just as they please." In *Dark Eden*, this even applies, on a meta-level, to the emergence of history itself.

In reflecting upon its own narrative process, *Dark Eden* forcibly calls our attention to the way that the "origin" it recounts is already tainted – or at the very least, already fictional. It is not a true origin, since it derives from the previous history of human beings on Earth. There is no true origin, therefore, but only an imperfect repetition – or perhaps an *adaptation*, using this word as much in the literary sense as in the biological one. The story of human beings adapting to the somewhat different conditions of life on the dark planet Eden is itself an adaptation, under different circumstances, of a story that is already old, already played out on Earth. As a work of science fiction, *Dark Eden* views both the "primitive" and the "advanced" states of human-kind retrospectively, through a kind of inverted extrapolation. It gives us a future that recapitulates our past, and for which our own future is already its own vanished past.

How does all this relate to our present historical moment, the time in which *Dark Eden* was written, and in which it is now being read? The science fiction writer Kim Stanley Robinson suggests that

science fiction works by a kind of double action, like the glasses people wear when watching 3D movies. One lens of science fiction's aesthetic machinery portrays some future that might actually come to pass; it's a kind of proleptic realism. The other lens presents a metaphorical vision of our current moment, like a symbol in a poem. Together the two views combine and pop into a vision of History, extending magically into the future.

(Robinson 2019)

Following this logic of double action, we might well say that John Redlantern prefigures (or should I say *postfigures*?) what we currently call an entrepreneurial type, somebody like Steve Jobs or Mark

Zuckerberg, whose *modus operandi* is to "move fast and break things" (Taplin 2017). And we might equally well say that David Redlantern prefigures what we currently call a populist, quasi-fascistic demagogue, somebody like Donald Trump, who loudly demands the restoration of old values, but does not really believe in them, and really aims only at untrammeled domination. Several recent social theorists, most notably Melinda Cooper, have argued that the neoliberal cult of innovation and the neoconservative cult of the family and tradition are in fact mutually interdependent, two sides of the same coin (Cooper 2017). *Dark Eden* envisions the joint emergence (or better, re-emergence) of these two tendencies, co-dependent precisely in their hostility to one another. Beckett's outlook is grim; but in accounting for the highly contingent development of the two sides, he offers us a multidimensional "vision of History," of the sort that Robinson calls for. Even as *Dark Eden* recapitulates the steps that helped lead to our actual deplorable social configuration, it helps us to realize that this configuration is not given once and for all. The way we live now, just like the way they come to live in Eden, requires particular conditions of emergence. This means that there may also be particular conditions under which it could be transformed, or pass away.

Is there truly no alternative (to cite Margaret Thatcher's infamous phrase) to the bifurcation envisioned by *Dark Eden*? In passing, Beckett at least lets us glimpse two versions of a less hierarchical, and less exploitative way of life after the fall of primitive communism. One of these is the vision of Tina Spiketree, who feels – as strongly as John does – the need to escape from the stifling conservatism of Family, but who also objects to what she rightly sees as the noxious consequences (gender hierarchy, private ownership, and authoritarianism) of John's charismatic form of leadership.

The other divergent vision is expressed in the person of John's cousin, Jeff Redlantern. Jeff is a clawfoot, which means that he cannot walk very easily, or very far. Due to his disability, Jeff is spared from the expectations of normative masculinity that mark both John and David:

Other boys became men by putting on the masks of men, and shutting out of their heads all the things that didn't fit with their masks, but if you were a clawfoot no one expected you to wear that mask, or to shut those things out of your head. That was why I *saw* things that other people didn't see.

As a result, other people in Eden find Jeff a bit strange. We might even say – to use a term that applies in our own world, but that is unknown in Eden – that Jeff is a person who is located somewhere along the autistic spectrum. This is manifested in various ways. For one thing, he never tires of the wonder of sheer existence: he frequently cries out things like "We're here! ... This is happening. We really are here!" Tina remarks that Jeff is "interested interested in everything"; and even John recognizes that Jeff is able "to see the wide world beyond" what everyone else pays attention to. He will "never settle for seeing only one side of a thing." Jeff is always aware that there are many other perspectives besides his own; he reflects that, even if he were to die, "the world would still have had lots of other eyes to see through ... even when someone died, the secret awakeness that had been looking out of their eyes would always still be there."

Thanks to this open sensibility, Jeff is quite original and inventive. It is he, for instance, who first domesticates the woollybucks, large herbivores on Eden. He is able to empathize with these animals, despite their alien weirdness that repels everyone else. By riding on the back of a woollybuck, Jeff is able to compensate for his disability, traveling far distances without having to walk. Despite his inventiveness, however, Jeff has none of John's mania about innovation for its own sake, and none of John's ambitions to be a leader, and to manipulate and control other people.

In the second and third volumes of the trilogy, we learn that, after the events recounted in *Dark Eden*, both Tina and Jeff seceded from John's group, and founded their own communities on more egalitarian lines. Their survival is quite tenuous, however. In the course of these volumes, Jeff's people are not far enough away to escape subordination to the Davidfolk. Half Sky, the community founded by Tina, is widely scorned by the patriarchal Davidfolk and Johnfolk. It sounds like a utopia; men and women remain on equal terms, and leaders are chosen democratically. But Half Sky only survives for the moment thanks to its geographical distance from the other societies of Eden. In the long run, it remains under military threat.

Probably all speculation – not just about human origins, but also about potential future directions – requires a certain degree of reversion and recapitulation. Just as the people of Eden cannot possibly imagine what bright sunlight is really like, so there are doubtless conditions that we are unable to conceive adequately. Most likely, we are not even able to grasp how off the mark we are. As a result, we are all too often compelled to fall back upon the very formulations that have already disappointed us. This is perhaps why Fredric Jameson ultimately concludes that the utopia imagined by science fiction can have no positive content, but can only be "a radical break or secession ... from political possibilities as well as from reality itself" (Jameson 2005). Chris Beckett touches upon this dilemma in his own way, by giving us a speculative fabulation of the very limits of fabulation.

Chapter 7
Splendor and Misery

Splendor and Misery is a 2016 album by the experimental hip hop group clipping. (consisting of Daveed Diggs, William Hutson, and Jonathan Snipes). The group describes this work, on its *Bandcamp* page, as "an Afrofuturist, dystopian concept album that follows the sole survivor of a slave uprising on an interstellar cargo ship, and the onboard computer that falls in love with him" (clipping. 2016). We might say that *Splendor and Misery* is a space opera, in a more literal sense of the term than usual. The narrative fits the common definition of the genre, as it unfolds in the far future, and involves an adventure on a starship in interstellar space. But this science fictional storyline is largely conveyed through musical (or more broadly, sonic) means. Also, most of the album's tracks are more concerned with exploring the wider ramifications of the story, than with elaborating the plot in detail. In this way, it is quite different from a written science fiction narrative. Such reflective storytelling in music, with rapping and singing plus noise plus a few music videos, makes for something like the twenty-first-century equivalent of nineteenth-century opera. *Splendor and Misery* is entirely devoid of Wagnerian grandiosity; it is quite short (37 minutes), and – despite its cosmic implications – it is intimate in scope. But much as Wagner's operas do, albeit from a vastly different political and cultural position, *Splendor and Misery* offers us a mythically resonant critique of modernity.

Splendor and Misery takes place on a starship whose "cargo" consists of slaves. These prisoners have been "selected for their strength"; this probably means that they are destined to serve as cannon fodder in a war zone. But before any destination is reached, the prisoners rebel against their servitude. Almost all of them are killed in the course of the uprising, together with "the crew and other passengers." It seems that the starship's AI is to blame for these deaths; fearing "a total loss of control," it causes sedatives and poisons to be "pumped through all the vents" of the ship.

However, one of the slaves survives the massacre. He succeeds in escaping confinement, commandeering the ship, and "setting a new course." Significantly, we never learn this survivor's name; he is referred to only by his slave classification, Cargo number 2331. No matter how far he goes, we are told, "he is still a runaway slave and so lonely." His "gift of freedom" is only a negative one: a *freedom from*, but not a *freedom to*. The only thing he can do is continue to run away; he cannot help being "paranoia prone," for "he knows they're coming for him" no matter what. He has "no destination" for his flight, and no companions to share it with; in such circumstances, "his survival is paramount, there is no other objective."

The album's scenario designedly recalls the historical Middle Passage, when kidnapped Africans were transported by ships across the Atlantic, in order to be sold as slaves in the New World. Today, the Middle Passage functions as a crucial point of reference for Afrofuturist efforts both to understand the actual history of Black oppression, and to imagine alternative histories and futures that would be free from this oppression. What would it mean to be abducted by cruel, strange-looking aliens, who showed no mercy or empathy, but who overwhelmed you with their powerful military and carceral technology, dragged you away from your home, and put you to work in a hellish new world? It sounds like a science fiction scenario, but it actually happened: as Kodwo Eshun puts it, "slavery functioned as an apocalypse experienced as equivalent to alien abduction" (Eshun 2003). Chattel slavery in the New World was no aberration; we can no longer ignore its central role in establishing capitalist modernity as we know today (see, e.g., Beckert and Rockman 2016).

Eshun further reminds us that those kidnapped and enslaved Africans were the first moderns: the first people to experience the real conditions of existential homelessness, alienation, dislocation, and dehumanization that philosophers like Nietzsche would later define as quintessentially modern ... Slavery functioned as an apocalypse experienced as equivalent to alien abduction ... Afrofuturism therefore stages a series of enigmatic returns to the constitutive trauma of slavery in the light of science fiction.

(Eshun 2003)

In this way, *Splendor and Misery* returns to the scene of the Middle Passage, and also to the long (and often suppressed) history of slave rebellions in the New World. The album fabulates an alternative future history by extrapolating from actual past traumas. When Afrofuturism takes up past events, projecting them into the far future, it revises and replays those events, in order to give them different – and less dire – outcomes. The Black Quantum Futurist movement today envisions "creative futures" as a way to "reach back to redefine the present and the past" (Phillips 2015). This is the utopian, liberatory side of Afrofuturism. At the same time, however, Afrofuturist speculation forcibly reminds us how deeply this history of oppression still weighs upon the world today. The United States of America has never made reparations for the slavery and genocide that were instrumental to its founding, and that still lie at the roots of its prosperity. The traumatic events of the past are not dead and buried; rather, they continue to shape the actualities of the present, and to infect our visions of the future. This is the dystopian side of Afrofuturism, resonating with the philosophical project of Afro-pessimism (cf. racked & dispatched 2017). *Splendor and Misery* partakes of both these tendencies. Cargo number 2331 frees himself from bondage; but he is still marked as a fugitive, and he is unable to create a new life elsewhere.

The way into *Splendor and Misery* is through its aggressively disruptive soundscape. Most of the album is dissonant and noisy. Hutson and Snipes' electronically generated soundtrack includes melodies and beats such as we would expect from a hip hop album; but it also features nerve-racking low-frequency drones, together with static, distortion, feedback, and other sorts of unpitched sound. This noise sometimes works, in traditional musical ways, to accompany, and emotionally inflect, the album's rapping and singing. But just as often, the noise interferes with the vocals: it plays over the words and threatens to drown them out.

We can hear this right at the start of *Splendor and Misery*. On the opening track, "Long Way Away (Intro)," the performance artist Paul Outlaw sings a plaintive verse that introduces the themes of the entire album:

I'll follow the stars when the sun goes to bed
Till everything I've ever known is long dead
I can't go back home 'cause I want to be free
Someone tell the others what's become of me.

I am quoting the lyrics here as if they were clearly audible; but in fact, they are difficult to distinguish. Outlaw's voice is electronically altered; it is so distorted that it sounds as if he were singing from inside a closet, or through a low-fidelity megaphone. And his words are smothered by a wall of sound, consisting of static together with a rumbling drone that suggests the roar of airplane engines (or perhaps I should rather say, in this context, the roar of starship engines). We are barely able to extract the signal from the noise; the message seems to have been broadcast from a great distance, and under conditions of duress. This tells us that the starship is indeed, as the track's title suggests, "a long way away," lost in the vast emptiness of interstellar space.

Outlaw's opening song-fragment is reprised a number of times in the course of the album. We hear it at the end of the fifth track, "Wake Up," leading into the sixth track's full-length choral version of "Long Way Away." A few tracks later, the haunting melody is repeated again, without the lyrics, in "Long Way Away (Instrumental)." And we hear the fragment one last time, with slightly different lyrics, at the start of the final track, "A Better Place." Each time, we are reminded that home, companionship, and redemption are not available to Cargo number 2331 any longer.

What is it really like to be a long way away, to be permanently exiled from home? This is the emotional and conceptual focus of the album. Cargo number 2331 "dare not stay long" in any one location, for fear of capture. In our relativistic universe, distances in space are also passages of time. If you travel at close to the speed of light, what might seem to you like a short interval of time corresponds to an immense duration for the people you left behind. A near-light-speed voyage, like the one recounted in *Splendor and Misery*, is therefore also a kind of time travel. But this traversal of time goes only in one direction: it hurls you irreversibly into the far future. The "ship's clocks count millennia," we are told, as it presses its "course relentlessly forward." Even if you were able to return to your spatial starting point after such a voyage, so much time would have passed that everyone and everything you knew from before your departure would be long gone. This dislocation of time and space is the objective correlative of Cargo number 2331's existential sense of exile.

The speaker of "Long Way Away (Introduction)" laments that "everything I've ever known is long dead." He "can't go back" to a home that has been destroyed. The price of freedom is eternal exile and eternal solitude. The only escape from slavery is into a far future when it no longer exists – in part because, by that time, human society itself might well no longer exist. *Splendor and Misery* recounts, almost in spite of itself, a mad flight, a vast displacement, an irreversible journey away from any point of origin and from any form of community. This is not an exciting nomadic adventure, but a harsh necessity. Unable to return, the speaker begs us, out of his nearly incomprehensible displacement in space and time, to at least preserve his memory, and to connect him, at least notionally, with other people: "tell the others what's become of me." In effect, this desperate request sets out the task that the album as a whole seeks to accomplish.

Musical performance is usually thought to heighten our sense of the present moment: it unfolds as an extended duration, during which musicians and listeners alike are enveloped in the same atmosphere of sound. This is all the more so with music organized around rhythmic call and response, as in the African-American tradition. The modern technologies of broadcasting and recording detach the musical performance from its point of origin; but this is often said to extend the musical sense of heightened presence. Broadcast allows for sonic events to be received all over the world in real time; recording allows the sound to resonate with full effect in other places and at other times.

But *Splendor and Misery* undermines this common presumption of sonic presence and simultaneity. It proposes a more alienated, or deconstructive, understanding of sound. Throughout the album, we are reminded of the gap between broadcast and reception, not to mention the loss of fidelity in the process of reproduction. There is no hope of call and response when the singer is isolated, and the sonic event is stretched out and dispersed. Cargo number 2331 desperately cries out for some sort of solidarity:

So drop the message ...
Get at me, my brothers, my sisters, get at me
Where are you? (Interlude 03 – Freestyle)

But he gets no answer to his call. There is no community out in the reaches of deep space; and hence no reciprocity or response. The atmosphere of noise and interference corresponds to a blockage on the level of narrative. As Nadine Knight observes, this is quite different from what happens in earlier, more optimistic, Afrofuturist works. *Splendor and Misery* is quite bleak; it "cannot imagine a world where the slave family can escape as a unit, where a home can be made among the emancipated" (Knight 2018).

At one point, the album drops a poignant memory of life before abduction and enslavement:

Happiness is waiting at your door
In a sleek black dress and a kiss that says "hello"
And a thick black mess and a mom that says "don't go."

But the point of this reminiscence is that it presents a past that cannot be recovered. Cargo number 2331 *did* go away, for whatever (voluntary or involuntary) reasons. And now there is no way for him to return.

The album makes us hear, as it were, the very distance – and especially the time delay – separating the emission of the sounds from their reception. As Daveed Diggs raps at one point, "what if everything was at the wrong time?" The album ponders this question throughout. We might say that Cargo number 2331's rebellion unavoidably happens at the wrong time: rather than being a historical event, it is only possible as a disruption of the (linear, progressive) order of history. Lacking a collective dimension, it cannot create a new reality, one that would have ongoing historical consequences. This slave rebellion is only a gap in the record. No matter what Cargo number 2331 does, "time will not afford him/Any cover, any pardon." The narrative cannot be brought to any satisfying conclusion. We have no direct, real-time access to the album's science fiction story; we can only experience it in delayed and distorted fragments. The album presents itself to us as a hazardous, incomplete, long-distance, time-lagged, and one-way-only *transmission*.

Traditional communication theory is all about decoding transmissions; that is to say, "reproducing at one point either exactly or approximately a message selected at another point" (Shannon 1949). The aim is to extract a meaningful signal, isolating it from the background noise that accompanies, surrounds, and obscures it. *Splendor and Misery* plays with, and reminds us of, this process. There are several ciphers embedded in the album. The track "Interlude 02 (Numbers)" consists entirely of a distorted voice, almost drowned out by static, delivering a coded message in the NATO phonetic alphabet, where each word stands for a letter: "Foxtrot, Uniform, Whiskey, Romeo,/Whiskey, Charlie, Oscar, X-Ray," and so on. The sequence spelled out here is not in itself intelligible; apparently, it is a Vigenère cipher, the key to which is given in "Air 'Em Out." That track, in turn, also features clicks that give a message in ASCII code. There is also a sequence of Morse code dots and dashes embedded in the noisy background of "True Believer." And the final track on the album, "A Better Place," gives us some cryptic numerical coordinates. Online commentators have cracked all these ciphers, though the results are not tremendously informative (Kupermintz 2016; u/opheres 2018; afloweroutofstone 2019).

Despite the existence of these particular ciphers, however, we cannot find a clear message in *Splendor and Misery* by simply extracting the signal from the noise, or by isolating the lyrics from the rest of the sounds. As Diggs raps at one point, "the life binary in Morse code/Ain't really a life, right?" There is no way of reducing the album to information or code, no way of separating its ideas from its emotional atmosphere of distress and confusion. The album does not have a core message content that could somehow be extracted from the noise, and reproduced "either exactly or approximately" at another location and in another time. For dislocations of time and space are necessarily inscribed within it. We must grasp the album *as* transmission, by attending as much to the noise itself, and to the time lag that it implies, as to the angry and melancholy lyrics. *Splendor and Misery* in effect dramatizes a point made by the philosopher Michel Serres. All messages are accompanied by static and interference, Serres tells us, and the process of understanding them is therefore recursive and interminable. The noisy interruption becomes a crucial component of the very signal that it interrupts. The message can only be understood when we include the difficulties and even the outright failures of its reception (Serres 1982).

In fact, the mere *presence* of ciphers at various points in the album is more important than the particular messages they convey. Daveed Diggs says in an interview that "slave spirituals" in the antebellum South often contained "coded messages about how to get north." But he immediately adds that, on a deeper level, "the philosophy behind them was about transcending place. They were about home actually being in the unknown" (White 2016; cited in afloweroutofstone 2019). The encrypted songs in *Splendor and Misery*, like those in slave times, point to a metaphysical longing for home – something that goes well beyond the codes' actual messages. How do you find your home when it is unknown, or long lost, and when the place you actually inhabit is a site of captivity?

Diggs' reference to slave spirituals also helps to explain why the album is punctuated, on several tracks, with singing by the male *a cappella* gospel group Take 6. Their sweet, melancholy harmonies, and even their lyrics, are designedly reminiscent of old slave spirituals. Take 6's vocals thus cut against the grain of the album's otherwise ubiquitous noise and dissonance. Sometimes, as in "True Believer," these voices sing a yearning chorus about "going home" against a continuing background of static. But on other tracks – "Long Way Away" and "Story 5" – their singing is unaccompanied by noise or instruments; as Ruben Ferdinand puts it, this singing is "pristine, perfect in dreamlike vividity" (Ferdinand 2016). "Long Way Away" is mournful but accepting; it reminds us that "there's no use in crying/No reason to wait." But it also pointedly asks us to "pray that your children/Do not sing this song." The cycle threatens to continue, repeating itself from out of the past, and into the far future.

"Story 5" stands out among the tracks sung by Take 6, because it is the only song on the album that neither forms part of the far future story, nor simply recalls the past of slavery. Rather, despite its elegiac tone, it seems to be set in the present moment. The song tells us about an empathetic woman named Grace, loved by everyone around her, who is apparently murdered when she attempts to expose malfeasance at the factory where she works. This melodious track also expresses a yearning for home that is unfulfilled: the verses recount her gory death ("severed limbs and blood"), while the chorus asks, "Oh Grace, won't you come back home?" "Story 5" thus combines the past of slavery (in its melody and general feel) with the present of continuing oppression (in its narrative content), posing both in implicit relation to the album's projected future. Take 6's *a cappella* singing evokes a sense of sentimental loss that feels quite different from – but that is strictly correlative to – the harsh alienation expressed through the album's noise.

In counterpoint to this static that interferes with communication – what we might call the album's *negative noise* – *Splendor and Misery* also offers us a lot of *positive noise*: bangs, clicks, burbles, groans, and other such sounds, as well as the frequent rumbling drones. As the album's

Bandcamp statement says, there is "music in the ship's shuddering hull and chirping instrument panels," with "rhythms produced by its engines and machinery." These electronic sounds create "an imaginary sonic map of the ship's decks, hallways, and quarters." The starship's creaks and rustlings give us a powerful sense of place, and of materiality. The ship's massive sonic presence is both bountiful and precarious. The sound reminds us of how zealously it protects Cargo number 2331, both from the vacuum, silence, and extreme cold just beyond its thin walls, and from the other vessels pursuing him. Yet this busy noise also suggests that the machinery is not quite running smoothly, and that it may even be on the verge of breaking down. We are all too aware that the starship is pushing things to the limit, as "the navigations are failing, having traveled further than before." In any case, hearing what one track calls "the echoes of the bowels of this floating metal hull" is crucial to our grasp of the story.

Daveed Diggs' rapid-fire rapping mostly interacts with this positive noise. Diggs uses his voice in many different ways throughout the album, shifting among multiple roles in the narrative. At times he speaks in the persona of the starship AI, his voice a fast monotone, his diction rather stilted ("The Breach"). At other times, he speaks in the voice of Cargo number 2331, either with frantic and disjointed mumbling (the two brief freestyle tracks, "Interlude 01" and "Interlude 03," and perhaps also "Break the Glass"), or else overtly expressing his aggression ("Air 'Em Out"). And at still other times, Diggs' voice cannot be identified with either of the characters in the drama; instead, he offers a more abstract and distanced sort of commentary on the story. On these tracks, his voice often adopts more obviously mannered vocal rhythms ("True Believer"); or it varies from sardonic reproach to exasperation to a concerned whisper ("Baby Don't Sleep"). Diggs also code-switches continually, moving between standard English and African-American Vernacular.

Diggs' lyrics are always carefully stylized, even when they seem most frenetic. They are filled with allusions to works by other hip hop and pop artists, ranging from Kendrick Lamar to The Notorious B.I.G. to Carly Simon. They also reference a number of science fiction writers: Octavia Butler, N. K. Jemisin, Ursula Le Guin, M. John Harrison, and above all Samuel R. Delany. In fact, the name of the album is derived from Delany's title *The Splendor and Misery of Bodies, of Cities* – the announced but never actually written sequel to his space opera *Stars in My Pocket Like Grains of Sand* (Delany 1984). Delany derived his title, in turn, from Balzac's delirious social realist novel, *Splendors and Miseries of Courtesans*. The lineage here is clear. The great ambition of Delany's space opera, much like that of Balzac's novels, is to perform what Fredric Jameson calls "cognitive mapping" (Jameson 1991): that is to say, to analyze how particular individuals find themselves embedded in, and constrained by, social and economic networks that far exceed their grasp. *Stars in My Pocket* is concerned – among many other things – with the continuing legacy of slavery and genocide in a highly technologized and ostensibly cosmopolitan culture. Although clipping.'s own album is too short and compressed to do this sort of analysis – instead of cognitive mapping, it recounts a voyage into unmapped realms – it presumes our acquaintance with the deep background of the slavery-capitalism nexus.

We first hear Diggs' voice when he explicitly takes on the persona of the "Mothership" – that is to say, the starship's AI – on the second ("The Breach") and third ("All Black") tracks of the album. The AI reports what at first it sees as merely "a small anomaly." This is in fact the start of the slave rebellion. In the course of the track, the AI becomes increasing concerned with the revolt. It offers to take suppressive action, but it still "requires an approval code from the administration" in order to do so. Then it warns – its sense of urgency still expressed in an almost comedically bureaucratic prose – that "it cannot easily be overstated the importance of alacrity/In acting out the task commanded." Finally, when it is already too late, the AI asks to "send security immediately over to the gate." Behind these declarations, we hear the roar of the starship's ordinary functioning. But at a certain point, as the AI completely loses control, this drone gives way to sounds of glass being shattered, stuff being smashed and broken, fighting, and danger sirens going off.

The AI only has a limited understanding of human beings. It grasps motivation and action from the outside, using sensors to monitor the physiological state of its human inhabitants. As the rebellion heats up, the AI notes a "spiking in the pulse of a member of the cargo," followed by a "critical" level of "endorphins that are often linked to violence," and then a "rage in the nervous system." Once Cargo number 2331 has taken over, the AI observes his facial expression and bodily posture in addition to these somatic indicators; thus it observes that "his vitals read normal but his face reads murderous." The AI still fails to understand habitual human actions, however, as when it watches Cargo number 2331 say grace ("he insists on speaking passages before he eats") or take a shower (which seems to the AI to be "a ritual of some sort"). It also describes how Cargo number 2331

babbles beautifully
Of Babylon and enemies and foes ...
... rapping to himself
Until his vocal cords collapse.

("All Black Everything")

This effectively conveys the man's rage and despair to us, while showing that the AI itself still doesn't quite get it.

Despite this incomplete understanding – or perhaps because of it? – the AI gradually falls in love with Cargo number 2331. The escaped prisoner has "unlocked something new" in the ship; in freeing himself, he has also freed the AI from its own bondage to its imperial owners. The AI now finds capacities within itself that it was never aware of before: "the metal's being moved into a thing it doesn't do." There's an amicable and even erotic dimension to the ship's new feelings:

If only he realized this ship is more than metal.
There's friendship in the wiring, and so lonely.
If only he realized this ship has many levels.
There's pleasure in here hiding, come find it.

("All Black Everything")

As Nadine Knight rightly observes, the ship's love for its human passenger offers us "a refreshing twist" on the usual space opera narrative, one that "gestures toward rich readings of posthuman romance and genderqueer readings" of the relations between human and machine (Knight 2018).

But alas, this queer utopian promise does not come to fulfillment. Conditions are just too grim. Cargo number 2331 does not seem to understand the AI's overtures, and in any case does not respond to them: this is yet another instance of unreciprocated messages. Evidently, Cargo number 2331 has only a functional understanding of the starship; he never asks it for anything more than to "turn on the light" or to provide him with some "beats." Whatever cyborg dreams the AI may entertain, the album's focus remains on the finitude and vulnerability of Cargo number 2331's all-too-human body. "Flesh is weaker than the metal," after all; "the body can only take so much." While "circuitry" is "serviceable" for many purposes, "your sinews are more intuitively designed for dance." But is dancing even possible in these extreme circumstances? "The odds of the body/Making it through and surviving the gravity shift" are extremely slim. And again,

your body is bone marrow
And blood can never be trusted
It won't last to the nearest
Destination ...

("Baby Don't Sleep")

The AI's love for Cargo number 2331 is explored on the third track of the album, "All Black." This track starts with the Mothership reporting the slave rebellion and requesting assistance. But by the end, the ship instead demands safe passage for itself and its passenger: "This love will be defended at all costs, do not fuck with it." As it depicts this reversal of attitude, the track rings the changes upon multiple meanings of the repeated words "all black everything." This phrase was initially used in Jay-Z's 2009 song "Run This Town," where it refers to Jay-Z's style as an emblem of his Black nationalist (and capitalist) aspirations. The phrase has subsequently "become a certified Hip Hop meme" (Genius.com 2009). Most notably, Lupe Fiasco's 2011 song "All Black Everything" recounts a "dream" of a utopian world in which Black people are free and able to flourish, because the Middle Passage never happened: "there were no slaves in our history,/Were no slave ships, were no misery" (Genius.com 2011). In the song by clipping., which instead imagines an escape from the Middle Passage, "all black everything" still implies Black liberation; but it also refers (among other things) to the void of interstellar space, to the mental state of Cargo number 2331, with his rage and his inability to imagine any future, and even to the Abyss of the AI's own inhuman consciousness.

Since there is no place of safety, and "nowhere to arrive to," there can be no such thing as a happy ending (or even a definitively unhappy ending) to the story of *Splendor and Misery*. Cargo number 2331 tries to convince himself that his "sense of loneliness [is] the price of paying for a new beginning." But even this hope is precarious. For he knows that

The chance that he ever reaches any place
Suitable to support life in his lifetime's pretty low
And the chances of him of ever seeing anybody
That he knows are even lower.

("Wake Up")

Rather than being able to find someplace to start over, therefore, Cargo number 2331 has to keep on moving. "Staying is surrendering"; no matter where he "pit-stops," he "dare not stay long." You "can't shake what you've done/No matter how far you outrun it"; and so the only option is to keep traveling at full speed through the interstellar void.

Since this voyage is interminable, the story of Cargo number 2331's lonely escape, and of the AI's thwarted love for him, cannot be brought to any sort of conventional narrative conclusion. *Splendor and Misery* works instead with a different, more oblique, mode of storytelling. The album's later tracks do not forward the narrative, so much as they offer a variety of perspectives on what is really an unresolvable situation. For instance, "True Believer" and "Air 'Em Out" both contain images of war, mass murder, and mass abduction, the very reality from which Cargo number 2331 is trying so desperately to escape.

Several other tracks concern the AI's effort to rouse Cargo number 2331 from his state of insensibility and despair. On the fourth track, it desperately calls on him to "Wake Up." On the twelfth track, it tries to get him to "Break the Glass" as one does in order to push an emergency button; on this track the phrase "wake up" is repeated over and over. And on the fourteenth track, it exhorts him, both roughly and gently, to stay alert: "Baby Don't Sleep." But what is gained by these returns to full awareness? Nothing can compensate for the dead-end bleakness of Cargo number 2331's situation. On "Wake Up," the AI's assurance that it will "be right here when you wake up" is transformed into the disquieting sense that, due to the starship's "jumps" through hyperspace, "there'll be no here when you wake up." On "Break the Glass," with its desperate call for an impossible connection, we get the ominous suggestion that "you already know they can't hate if they don't ever wake up." And in "Baby Don't Sleep," the loss of everything familiar, together with the fact of "no destination," seems to lead to cosmic nihilism:

Nothing is familiar
So the strange become the family
Analogies are old and useless
When was the last time you had a tree
For reference or for reverence?

Three of the album's tracks have associated music videos: "True Believer," "Air 'Em Out," and "Baby Don't Sleep." But these videos do not illustrate the album's overall narrative; they, too, are situational, devising indirect analogies for the torturous "bouts of stasis" to which Cargo number 2331 is prone. The words of "Air 'Em Out" suggest a violent revenge fantasy, full of military threats, as if Cargo number 2331 were himself to go to war against the warmakers who kidnapped and drafted him. But the music video for the track, directed by Carlos Lopez Estrada, instead suggests the underlying futility of the whole situation. Diggs, dressed in what looks like a flight uniform, sits at a table furnished with an old-style telephone, a desk lamp, and a few other items. He swallows pills from a medicine bottle, washing them down with liquid he drinks through a straw. Periodically, the objects on the table shake as if in an earthquake, and then rise up toward the ceiling (as might happen in the weightlessness of outer space). Diggs responds each time by trying to slap the objects back down to the table. (He does not seem to be affected by weightlessness.) He also grasps at pills floating through the air, and swallows them. At one point during the shaking, the screen goes black; after a few seconds, the image returns, but now seen through a night vision camera that gives everything a sickly green hue. Finally, the table itself rises up into the air; Diggs pushes it violently back down to the floor, and then slowly backs out of the room, while continuing to glance at the table with suspicion. The video does not give a literal depiction of weightlessness, but it amply conveys the sense of dislocation and frustration that Cargo number 2331 might feel as a result of his exile.

Lopez Estrada's video for "True Believer" also juxtaposes the mundane and familiar with the inscrutability and alienation of outer space. The start of the video shows us an inner-city bodega ("American Deli Market") late at night, closed and deserted, trash bags in front of it on the sidewalk. The track's harsh beats, over a staticky drone, are matched with cuts to closer and closer views. As Diggs' rapping starts, an astronaut in full spacesuit and helmet (played by Paul Outlaw) begins to rise out of the bodega's basement. From here on, there are no more cuts: the camera follows the astronaut with a single continuing shot that moves upwards with him, but also gradually pulls back as he ascends.

At first, we are close enough to the astronaut's face to see him look at us imploringly from within his helmet, as if he were begging us for a sign of recognition that we cannot give him. He lip-syncs the words of longing for home that are sung by Take 6 in the chorus. The astronaut rises slowly, past the store and the tenement floors above it, and into the sky. Behind him, we see city lights shining in the distance, and then, finally, the dark sky with just a few stars. By this time the song has reached its coda; the beats are gone, and we only hear the drone, punctuated by distorted and synthesized voices. Now we are able to see the astronaut's whole figure, encased in his golden spacesuit, hanging in the void. But we are no longer able to make out his face beneath the helmet; we are just too far away.

As for the track's vocals, Diggs raps in a slow, measured cadence, matching the brutal beats. The first verse of "True Believer" gives us an apocalyptic vision of warfare, once again recalling the Middle Passage. "Ships/Made for cargo and death" strafe a planetary surface, and abduct everyone whom they have not killed:

To the sky with them all
Not a one left on land
Traded in for steel hauls ...

In the second verse, however, Diggs widens the scope of his narration. He gives us a mythical account of the creation of the world, and its endless strife. There are three original sibling gods, who "fight as siblings do." One of them poisons her brother "just to see what he would do." As a result, he "vomited the sun"; the rest of the world as we know it soon followed. The gods finally created "man of many hues"; but these first human beings did not long remain on an equal footing, since "the white one in the image of/A sickly god would get his dues" at everyone else's expense. This myth of white privilege is echoed at the very end of the track, when a synthesized voice mutters that "pale gods told me to my face ... the place I seek I never find."

The third verse of "True Believer" traces, in allegorical form, the invention of slavery and capitalism. "Man" (sic – evidently meaning the dominant group of white people) "makes time come to a standstill." As a result, a certain "race of beings" is able to place

Time inside other bodies so they could sell it
The one thing in the universe no one held yet ...

How do you sell something as abstract as time? When time is encased inside human bodies, these bodies become stores of value.

They contain minutes and hours, days and weeks, which can be released and appropriated in the form of periods of work. Time is no longer a concrete duration that one lives through, but rather an abstract, measured, and finite quantity that one must give up in order to survive. Masters can profit by extracting this embodied time: either they own human bodies outright and work them to death (chattel slavery), or else they put those human bodies to work in measured increments (wage labor). In either case, slaves and workers are forced to expend themselves, giving up their embodied time in return for mere subsistence (or sometimes, not even that).

Cargo number 2331 is himself a victim of this procedure:

Time and he are inseparable in his mind ...
He must carry the burden of being the one
That time chose ...

Even as an escaped slave, he is still bound to this capitalized time, and therefore still compelled to race the clock. It is only "when time stops," if it ever does, that "for him finally there can be rest." But can time ever stop for any of us, short of death? On "Baby Don't Sleep," the penultimate track on the album, there is still "no time for waiting." And even on the somewhat-upbeat final track, "A Better Place," Cargo number 2331's "time-bound conscience" is still apparently the one thing "that keeps him out pushing through nothing."

The music video for "Baby Don't Sleep" is far more abstract than the other two videos. It provides an appropriately harsh visualization of the scorched-earth, violently amelodic texture of the track. The video is directed by the multimedia artist Cristopher Cichocki, whose "visual experiments" involve "interference static, oscilloscopic wavelengths, and flicker-frame animation" (PIAS 2016). The track's sonic background consists in rhythmic pulses of static, white noise, and sonic events that sound like collisions, or like objects shattering into fragments. The video matches these rhythms with strobe cuts among abstract patterns of vertical and crisscross interference lines, flashes of what looks like decayed film stock, animations of patch cables attaching themselves to a huge mixing board, and the disappearing signal of a video screen as it is turned off.

When Diggs raps in this video, his face appears in extreme close-up. He lip-syncs the song while sunglasses cover his eyes. His image is usually presented in a black-and-white negative; sometimes it flashes positive for a moment, and other times the face-on image is replaced or supplemented by ghostly profiles facing inward from both edges of the screen. At still other times, the camera is so close that Diggs' lips nearly fill the screen. Diggs' image continually flickers, and often seems on the verge of dissolving into abstract patterns. Moreover, his image is almost never presented directly to the camera. Rather, it is layered behind various sorts of quickly pulsing lattice patterns and other obstructions, including wire-mesh fences, screens, strobe flashes, and rapidly alternating lines.

"Baby Don't Sleep" is lyrically as well as sonically the most abrasive track on the album. Diggs alternates between more declamatory and more metrical styles of rapping. His words caustically demolish all of the hopes, fears, and laments that have been expressed on previous tracks. Cargo number 2331's ideals – the things he yearns after, and believes in – are nothing more than self-inflicted, and indeed cripplingly self-congratulatory, delusions:

You call it god, or man, or woman
Love or hope, it's all the same
A nickel-bag philosophy, a beta boost inside a brain.

These are all consolations. They might make Cargo number 2331 feel better, in the same way a nickel bag of weed would. But they don't really change anything. They have no purchase upon the actuality of his situation. They explain away his oppression and his exile, without giving him any tools to deal with them.

Diggs issues a steady stream of bitter words, throughout the track. But he pauses, briefly, just before the pre-chorus, and then again before and during the chorus proper. (The pre-chorus and chorus come around twice in the course of the song.) The pre-chorus and chorus are also the only portions of the track that have any sort of toned sounds to them at all, rather than just unpitched noise. The pre-chorus reminds Cargo number 2331 yet again of the losses he has suffered, and of the emptiness of his hopes:

No home, you've been there
Clearly off safety
No destination
No time for waiting ...

And most importantly of all, perhaps: "saviors are fiction." Cargo number 2331 shouldn't expect any sort of redemption or restitution. Nobody is going to rescue him. But then, Diggs ends the pre-chorus poignantly rather than harshly, by evoking "memories fading like ghosts, ghosts." There is no cure for yearning and nostalgia, except to know that they too will fall apart, and vanish into oblivion.

After another pause, we get the chorus proper, which gives us the track's only hint of a respite. The chorus solely consists of repetitions of the title phrase "baby don't sleep." (Sometimes it is extended to "baby don't sleep too much.") At first, the phrase is repeated in Diggs' almost-singing voice; then it is repeated in a high-pitched, cartoony synthesized voice. But finally, after yet another brief pause, Diggs says "baby don't sleep" just once more – only this time in a whisper, and with no accompanying background noise. I want to say that this concluding whisper, with its note of tenderness and intimacy, entirely changes the overall feel of the song. It doesn't negate all the bitter scorn that came before; we are still in the heart of loneliness and loss. We also remain aware that much of Cargo number 2331's misery has been self-inflicted; as we recall from an earlier track, he "seems upset by that to which he is subjected/But convinced he brought it on himself." But even at this desperate moment, oblivion and exile also have much to recommend them – especially when the alternative, the society that Cargo number 2331 is fleeing from, is grounded in slavery, murder, and exploitation. "Baby don't sleep," and you may be able, knowingly, to embrace the "all black everything."

Indeed, clipping. suggests as much on its *Bandcamp* page for *Splendor and Misery*:

In a reversal of H. P. Lovecraft's concept of cosmic insignificance, the character finds relief in learning that humanity is of no consequence to the vast, uncaring universe. It turns out, pulling the rug out from under anthropocentrism is only horrifying to those who thought they were the center of everything to begin with. Ultimately, the character decides to pilot his ship into the unknown – and possibly into oblivion – instead of continuing on to worlds whose systems of governance and economy have violently oppressed him.

(clipping. 2016)

Isn't there something dishonest – or perhaps it would be better to say, symptomatic – about the way that Lovecraft conflates cosmic indifference with cosmic malice? On the one hand, Lovecraft's Old Ones appear to be no more concerned with (or even aware of) human beings than we are with the tiny organisms that we obliterate under our feet, unknowingly, with every step we take. But on the other hand, and at the same time, these figures are portrayed as willfully destructive, and actively hostile to (ostensibly civilized) humankind; this is what makes them grotesque objects of pagan worship, screens upon which Lovecraft projects all his racist fantasies. There is a nasty sleight of hand at work here, in the way that cosmic horror provides an alibi for Lovecraft's panicky clinging to white supremacy. Against this, Cargo number 2331 does well to take comfort in the evidence of a "vast, uncaring universe." After all – and in contrast to Lovecraft's neurasthenic upper-class white characters – he never thought that he was important, or at the center of things, in the first place. At the very least, the outer reaches of the cosmos are not pervaded with the parochial prejudices and injustices that actually prop up our own (white, patriarchal American) supposed cosmopolitanism and universalism.

These considerations help us to make sense of *Splendor and Misery*'s final track, "A Better Place." This song, unlike everything else on the album, features a corny, cheesy, upbeat melody – actually not much more than an extended cadence – that sounds like it is being played on a calliope, or some such carnivalesque instrument. Clashing with this, we hear Paul Outlaw's elegiac and heavily processed voice, singing "A Long Way Away," just like at the very start of the album; only this time, recalling the bitter experience of exile and isolation, Outlaw tells us to find nourishment in our very state of exile: "remember the darkness will show you the way."

After Outlaw's introduction, Diggs' voice enters the mix. His rapid rapping recapitulates many of the album's overall themes, from messages gone awry, to the oppressions of time (both when it passes away and when it lingers), to all the deprivations that Cargo number 2331 has suffered:

He's missing something pretty
He's missing where the air tastes gritty
He's missing the splendor and misery
Of bodies, of cities, of being missed ...

Here we have the loss of community, the loss of all sorts of experiences, both positive and negative (with a shout-out to Delany's lost novel), and finally the loss even of a certain feeling of loss ("being missed"). It's a problem, Diggs tells us, of "making the best of a universe/Far too expansive to cope with" – a universe that "he never chose" – while "the senses are numbed by emotional stresses." Cargo number 2331 (and anybody who follows in his footsteps) is a victim of "centuries/Of mistakes" that he cannot help internalizing; he "calls it history." We cannot erase the past, but must we remain bound by its constrictions? Diggs suggests that "species with memories longer" than ours "don't bother with sweating the old shit."

All the while, the relentlessly upbeat carnival music continues, and even gets thickened with occasional drum beats and synthesized arpeggiated chords. The track goes round and round, coming back repeatedly to a chorus that Diggs sings instead of speaks:

There must be a
Better place to
Be somebody
Be somebody else

In the course of this chorus, the aim of Cargo number 2331's quest slips from the fully positive "be somebody" (as in the old protest chant "I am somebody!") to the far more ambiguous "be somebody else" (implying a process of metamorphosis). We would do well to be suspicious of fixed identities here, given how the album's protagonist finds it so difficult to shake off his former identity as a slave, fixed by a number. He doesn't know what "something else" will be, and neither do we. But this at least means that something is open, and not already predetermined.

Similarly, to say that "there must be a better place" is to make a wishful assertion, and not to state a settled fact. No "better place" is actually known; the album has argued at great length that the likelihood of finding one is minuscule. Nevertheless, "there must be" such a place; for Cargo number 2331's very life is staked upon "the hope brought on by this belief." The force behind this "must be," therefore, is hypothetical and multiply mediated: an insistence founded upon a hope that is itself founded upon an unsubstantiated belief. As Diggs says earlier in the track, it is a "bet" made in the full knowledge that its "odds are ungodly."

We might say, following the typology that Kim Stanley Robinson adopts from Fredric Jameson, that this attitude – "there must be a better place" – is not directly (or "naively") utopian, so much as it is "anti-anti-utopian" (Robinson 2019). To continue this quest for a better place in spite of all the odds is to reject the ostensibly "realistic" assumption that "there is no alternative" (Margaret Thatcher's notorious slogan, cited by Fisher 2009), or that the world we know, with its oppression and exploitation, is the only world there is or ever can be. It is better – and indeed even safer – to "set up a random course" into the unknown than to stay with what is reliably oppressive and deadly.

The qualifications here do not negate the force of the assertion; just as the self-consciously acknowledged chintziness of the music does not erase how jubilant and celebratory it feels – all the more so in the face of the harrowing experiences that the album has put us through up to this point. If this is irony, it's not of the usual cynical sort. Rather, clipping.'s mode of irony allows them to actually say something positive and affirmative, without falling into the Disneyesque cheerfulness of so much mainstream culture. As members of the band put it in an interview,

Making the void and the infinite unknown a triumphant choice at the end of this record was the heated discussion of many a night while making this record ... the discussion was how to make it sound like piloting into a black hole feel like a powerful choice.

(Burns 2016)

At the end of "A Better Place," as the music thickens, with more insistent arpeggios and more active percussion, Diggs repeats the exhortation

Are you ready to go?
Are you ready to go yet?
Let's go!

until finally all we hear of his voice is "Go! Go! Go!" in the background, gradually fading out, while the music gets ever louder, thicker and dronier. This sound is dissonant because of all the overtones, but it still contains pitched notes rather than unpitched noise. This final minute of the album even has some of the emotional effect of an extended cadence at the end of Wagner's operas or other pieces of classical music. But as befits the science fiction storyline, not to mention clipping.'s overall aesthetic, *Splendor and Misery* ends, not with any sense of final resolution and (post-orgasmic) repose in the tonic key, but rather with the sound abruptly cut off while it is still going full blast.

Chapter 8
Proof of Concept

Gwyneth Jones' 2017 novella *Proof of Concept* (Jones 2017) takes place some 200 years from now, in the early twenty-third century. The book is about a world that is depressingly similar to our own, except that things have gotten progressively worse. It is also about the prospects of escaping from such a world, given that nothing can be done to salvage or reform it. The book's storytelling is extremely compressed; even favorable reviewers tend to complain that this "dense and clotted story" (of about 30,000 words) would be better if it were expanded to full-novel length (Kincaid 2017). But I think that Jones draws considerable power from the brutal concision and abruptness of her text. Indeed, she suggests in a blog entry that expanding the story to novel length would risk making it feel "padded-out" (Jones 2017a). *Proof of Concept*, in novella form, is brilliantly telegraphic in its brevity. It never tells us anything more than once, and it gives us only laconic hints of matters that we need to flesh out for ourselves. Things that might be major plot points in other texts are here passed over in a sentence.

Take how *Proof of Concept* evokes its twenty-third century media landscape. On the very first page of the novella, we are introduced to the media personality Da Jue, who is "not human, not even the holopresence of a human," but rather an avatar: a "data entity" based on "the input from a fantastically huge global audience: the statistical sum of its real-time response." Despite being entirely generated by the artificial intelligence system known as Global Audience Mediation (GAM for short), Da Jue is given a gendered pronoun ("he") and a physical appearance: "an absurdly eager face and a bouncy body in a smart suit," and wearing a "gaudy necktie." Da Jue is a hyperactive, caricatural

TV talk show host, with "crazily intense attention," but a short attention span. He speaks at one moment "with slightly mad enthusiasm," giggles the next at a supposed "naughty word," and relaxes at the prospect of "fun" the moment after that, winking and smirking to the audience all the while.

After this brief appearance, we do not encounter Da Jue again. But in his (simulated) person, Jones has effectively given us all we need to know about how the media work in the world of *Proof of Concept*. Televisual programming, watched both on flat screens and in holographic 3D displays, is global in reach, ubiquitous, and highly interactive and immersive. GAM varies in tone: "the global audience had many faces," so that even Da Jue can be "nonpatronizing" and factual at times, instead of cheerfully inane. But whatever its momentary mood, GAM's interface is implacable in its grasp. It is instantly responsive to the desires and reactions of "the masses" – but only because it molds those desires and reactions in the first place.

GAM works as an outlet for discontent, offering the spectacle of people "saying outrageous things and meaning nothing." In this way, it provides "crude, fake, freedom of speech for people who have none." But behind the scenes, GAM sets the limits of what is thinkable. It watches you far more carefully than you ever watch it; "your every little eye kick, choice, and contact" is collated as data, so that it can be either "monetized, or racked up against you." You have to watch out; if you say something that goes too far beyond the guidelines, you may be subjected to "cognitive remodeling, or even Vanishment." Cartoonish displays like that of Da Jue allow the "fantastically huge global audience" to not take GAM seriously, or even to dismisss it as "a bad joke." But beneath this easy disavowal, everyone is forced to recognize the media system's authority and power. Its judgments are final; it can make you or break you. When GAM comes calling, you had better maintain "a warm, happy expression"; and above all, "you must never say *no*."

Behind this media facade, living conditions are grim. "At least there are no more wars"; but nothing in this early twenty-third century world is free from "the vicious stranglehold of the One Percent." The superrich continue to profit (much as they already do today) at everyone else's expense. Not only do the One Percent control all the wealth; they are also able to live for hundreds of years, thanks to longevity treatments that nobody else can afford. This gives them an even greater sense of entitlement; such "super-post-lifespans ... do whatever comes into their heads and they just don't care. They have no consideration, no boundaries." There is an ever-increasing gulf between the One Percent and the rest of humanity.

Meanwhile, the political system continues to deteriorate, together with the climate:

Many great cities had been abandoned. All the oceans were rated dead or dying, and a frightening global percentage of agricultural land was useless. Almost the entire human population lived packed into the surviving cities, remodeled and densely stacked: the crumbling "megahives." Inside the Hives civilization survived, in a permanent state of moderate crisis. Outside them scavengers eked out short lives in the polluted "Dead Zones," or in raft clusters on the acidified oceans, while every remaining scrap of agricultural land was machine-tended, and trespassers punished with summary execution.

However horrific this situation may seem, it is scarcely more than a straightforward science fictional extrapolation from conditions that we already face today. In the globalized, neoliberal world of the early twenty-first century, democratic structures are eroding. All human activities are rapidly being financialized, so that profits can be extracted from them. Wealth is redistributed ever upwards. Property rights – especially those to so-called "intellectual property" – are rigidly enforced, no matter the human costs. Everything that we think, say, or do is recorded by governments and large corporations. Global warming and environmental pollution also continue unchecked, and these governments and corporations go out of their way to block any actions that might reduce them. We muddle through "in a permanent state of moderate crisis." The authorities continually improvise makeshift and provisional measures, while making it impossible to address deeper problems. Logically speaking, these sorts of conditions cannot be sustained forever; eventually we will reach some point of total system failure, and the economy and the environment will both come crashing down. But this moment of reckoning is continually being deferred.

Proof of Concept asks us to consider the consequences of an additional two centuries of such deferral. Some things have changed, obviously, in the world of the novella. For instance, nation-states as we know them today no longer exist; they have been superseded by private corporations that exert their power directly. An individual person may still be designated as a "Yank," "Brit," or "Nigerian"; but these terms no longer refer to political entities. "There are only three actual countries left in the world. MegaCorps East, which you call China, MegaCorps West, and the Dead Zones." The last of these really isn't a country at all, as it consists of people reduced to *bare life* (Agamben 1998): they have "no legal status," no homes, no property to speak of, and no recourse against rape and murder. They scavenge for the necessities of life in otherwise abandoned areas, full of chemical contamination and radioactivity; they are continually falling ill, and they die young.

The "hivizens," in contrast to the inhabitants of the Dead Zones, ostensibly belong to what is still called "civilization." This seems to mean that they have legal citizenship rights, and a minimal degree of protection; but the MegaCorps, together with GAM, control every aspect of their lives. Strict censorship is the rule: "in the Hives an offline archive was seriously illegal: everything had to be open to inspection." The dense urban aggregations of the Hives are considered to be "a big improvement on the situation they'd replaced" – perhaps fortunately, we are not told what that previous situation was. Nevertheless, the Hives are not really a success. They are "crumbling" at best; some of them have "started collapsing" physically already, and are "not being replaced." In the Hives, "supply collapses, power failures, and food riots" are common. "Diseases could not be relieved; quality of hivizen life was constantly being eroded."

The hivizens are often described as "docile" and law-abiding, at least in comparison to the scavengers in the Dead Zones outside. Yet "this didn't stop the masses from resenting their captivity"; there are frequent outbursts of "violent unrest ... explosive civil unrest." Uprisings continue to break out, "despite firm policing, constant surveillance, and intense Global Audience Mediation" – and even despite the fact that arrested "rioters" are "put in cold sleep" (which is to say, "medically induced comas") indefinitely. In the long run, however, such "revolts were just the breeding ground for another generation of corrupt hivizen politicians. They did no good at all." No matter what reforms are made in response to the uprisings, nothing really changes. Somehow in the end "only the MegaCorps and the One Percent benefited."

Outside the Hives, "the hopelessly polluted areas kept on growing." People no longer bother to talk about the "Climate Change Crisis"; presumably all the disruptive climate events that we worry about today (warming, sea level rise, desertification, frequent megastorms, mass extinctions, and so on) have already happened. Instead, people worry about the "Population Crisis." For "in the crazy world of superdense population" – and given the grossly uneven distribution of wealth – human numbers far exceed the planet's damaged carrying capacity. Even with high-tech automated agri-culture, "the global population could not be fed" any longer. In such circumstances, the only "good news" is that "global population fig-ures, though still a problem given the world's depleted resources, were at last significantly *falling*." But this still isn't happening fast enough; "nothing, as yet, was getting any better." Proponents of what is euphemistically called "Extreme Population Control" are waiting in the wings.

In order to limit population size, reproduction is discouraged in the world of *Proof of Concept*. "Rational M/F partners chose to be sterile ... unless they had a baby permit." Such permits are rationed by lottery; but even if you are lucky enough to obtain one, you probably will not be able to keep it. For "baby permits got monetized" quickly; people are often compelled to sell them "on the open market," in order "to pay for medical treatment or to service a debt." In other words, legally sanctioned childbearing is *de facto* limited to the One Percent, who have the wealth to pay for it. But the situation also has its "con-verse": "if the masses, who had no common sense, wanted to have multiple babies *without* the advantages secured by a permit, there was no way to stop them." Although "the fate of many unlicensed babies was dreadful," poor people are driven to have kids anyway. Deprived of money and hope, they are by definition irrational or devoid of common sense. They have nothing to gain from not having children, since their own lives are so miserable already.

There is at least one good consequence of this horrible situation. Because of the need to discourage population growth, unconventional, nonprocreative sexualities are widely accepted in the world of *Proof of Concept* – in a way that is only starting to be the case today. Nobody blinks an eye at a person's being nonbinary, using *they/their* as personal pronouns, and rejecting any patronymic last name; nor even at a person's being "trisex" (whatever that means). "Old-fashioned contraception" – birth control as we know it today – has been replaced by the easier and more efficient process of "reversible sterilization." In any case, most people, most of the time, have sex only in virtual reality; in this way, they avoid not only pregnancy, but also sexually transmitted diseases. VR sex is called "playtime": there is full sensory stimulation, without bodies ever actually touching one another. Apparently the physical simulation is good enough, or the experience is rich and satisfying enough, that "many singles ... had never experienced actual sex ... and did not feel deprived." Indeed, playtime allows for expanded possibilities; many people "like to change" gender and body type when having virtual sex, rather than presenting as just a replica of their physical selves.

It should be noted, however, that in the world of *Proof of Concept*, such expanded sexuality is only tolerated as an unavoidable emergency measure. There's plenty of sexual titillation on reality television; but there are also dire warnings about "the dangers of actual sex, the fear of misplaced conception and hideous disease." Playtime is an outlet for peoples' desires and emotions; but it is also a way of keeping those desires and emotions contained. The same is true for the other sorts of distractions easily available in early twenty-third century society: alcohol, cannabis, computer games, and exercise in the gym. Whatever passing amusements are available, the bottom line remains that "the MegaCorps mind-set wanted everything in opposition: Either/Or; Yes/No; On/Off; M/F. They hated fluidity, blur, and multiplicity."

 Proof of Concept describes a world in which it seems that, even as our technologies get more powerful, and our consumer options expand, nothing essential can ever change. We are still stuck, two hundred years later, in the structure of feeling that the late Mark Fisher called *capitalist realism*. This means that we are unable to believe in – let alone work to achieve – any alternative to the *status quo* of predatory capitalism; "it is easier to imagine the end of the world than it is to imagine the end of capitalism" (Fisher 2009). Things are terrible, but they will never get better. Nature and society alike will just continue to decay. Under the regime of capitalist realism, "there is no punctual moment of disaster; the world doesn't end with a bang, it winks out, unravels, gradually falls apart" (Fisher 2009).

 The persistence of capitalist realism in the world of the novella is, once again, a matter of straightforward extrapolation. Already today, in the early twenty-first century, the global rich – despite their propaganda to the contrary – know better than anyone else that we are on the verge of ecological catastrophe. But they see no point in spending money to alleviate the damage. Instead, the One Percent think that they will be able to tough it out, with their wealth and privileges intact. They place all their bets on the hope of "insulating themselves from a very real and present danger of climate change, rising sea levels, mass migrations, global pandemics, nativist panic, and resource depletion" (Rushkoff 2018) – whether by retreating into bunkers or by colonizing Mars.

 In *Proof of Concept*'s early twenty-third century, these avoidance plans remain largely intact, although they are starting to get frayed around the edges:

Even the "One Percent," the global rich, were feeling the heat … The One Percent saw a time coming – getting closer at speed – when there would be nowhere left to hide.

 In the world of the novella, there are no unspoiled places left on Earth where the superrich can build their bunkers. Their luxurious "Near Space Orbital Hotels" are enticing places to go for a vacation, but they only provide a temporary refuge. Moreover, they have come to realize that "conventional Space, long ago ideal for this role, was not the answer." Small human outposts have been established on the Moon, Mars, the asteroids, and even the moons of Jupiter; but conditions in such places are unappealingly "arduous and perilous." Life is even more precarious out there than it has become back on Earth. You don't escape a wrecked environment by moving to an even more innately hostile one. The opportunities for the further expansion of capital throughout the Solar System turn out to be extremely limited.

Under such desperate circumstances, "the people needed a dream," something that would allow them to continue "hoping for a better tomorrow." And the One Percent need new places to hide, not to mention new resources to extract, in order to fuel their endless pursuit of ever-greater profits. There is only one thing that can satisfy these cravings: what GAM calls, with its usual manufactured enthusiasm, "*The Great Escape!*" This is the fantasy of interstellar travel, something that science fiction has envisioned for a long time. Forget the Solar System; we have ruined its only habitable planet beyond repair. But maybe we can find pristine Earth-like worlds circling other suns. And maybe we can transplant ourselves to them, and extract wealth from them. For the masses, the Great Escape is a simple dream of

tickets out for ordinary people, to places where there was air to breathe. An unspoiled ecosystem and gravity to hold your feet down. Giant starships, mass emigration.

For the One Percent, however, the calculations are a bit more complicated. They still need a viable exit strategy, as well as new territories to exploit. Therefore they encourage speculation about the Great Escape, and pour their money into its realization. They are very interested in building a giant starship for themselves. But this is a carefully limited goal. Despite their propaganda, the One Percent will never spend the resources necessary to build starships for the billions of other people trapped on Earth. Their attitude in the world of the novella is much the same as the actual attitude of the superrich today. As long as they themselves can avoid damage, and continue to accumulate wealth, they are perfectly happy to leave everyone else behind. That is to say, they are unconcerned by the prospect of genocide. It is just what the economists call an externality: an unfortunate but easily dismissible side effect of doing business.

There are two aspects to the project of the Great Escape: the actual scientific research on the one hand, and the social preparations on the other. The former will lead nowhere without the latter. Dan Orsted, one of the key characters in *Proof of Concept*, is the "Great Popularizer": the showman/entrepreneur who spreads the gospel of the Great Escape. Dan is a "colorful, tremendously optimistic figure"; he has a background in "Near Space Design," and he has been to the Moon and Mars. But he is best known as a reality show host: he is the maestro of Very Long Duration Mission Training (VLDMT for short; or LDM for even shorter), a TV series that aims to simulate the conditions of long voyages into deep space. The show features a "crew" of people living together in close quarters for extended periods; it is broadcast 24/7:

Hivizens loved VLDMT. Dan's teams were always available: they couldn't get away! You could share their lives every moment – bitching and socializing, having group sex (on the adult-rated version), struggling with close-confinement issues, arguing about toilet paper.

But even though Dan runs VLDMT "like popular entertainment," he also insists that

his project was serious ... Every mission had an authentic, habitable exoplanet in its sights and showcased an authentic, theoretically doable means of interstellar travel.

In order "to finance his obsession" with interstellar travel, we are told, Dan even "hustled the One Percent into paying ridiculous sums for ludicrous *starship tickets.*" In other words, he is a successful con man. Or, in more polite language, he is a showman and a mediator. He never disappoints his audience; and he moves easily between the superrich who finance his projects, and the masses who avidly watch his shows.

As for the actual scientific research toward interstellar travel, it is done by a group led by the physicist Margrethe Patel. Margrethe is routinely acknowledged to be the greatest scientist of her time. Nonetheless, people regard her as "snooty"; she has "near-zero credibility" in GAM, because her "Big Science past" is "tarnished by failure." Margrethe is haunted by the "collapse of the Orbital Toroid project" – a "controversial hyperspace experiment" gone wrong – that had previously been the focus of her research. But the Great Escape offers her a new opportunity. Margrethe promises the One Percent that "she could build them a starship. That's how she got her funding."

In Jones' vision, early twenty-third century physics has still not found a theory of everything (and probably never will). Instead, we have "Post Standard Model Physics" (PSM), which – as its name implies – remains grounded in the standard model of particle physics that was established in the 1970s. PSM is still haunted by the tension between the irreconcilable theories of relativity on the one hand, and quantum mechanics on the other. Einstein is still right: strictly speaking, "there is no faster-than-light travel ... you can't get rid of travel time, the way people used to imagine, without cost." But the physicists in the novella are interested in the way that quantum entanglement (which Einstein unsuccessfully tried to dismiss as "spooky action at a distance") might offer a loophole, circumventing this hard limitation.

Jones states, in a blog entry discussing the science behind the novella, that "I always derive my science fiction from real, cutting edge science." Of course, this does not mean that *Proof of Concept* is literally scientifically accurate. But the novella is grounded upon the way that, as Jones puts it, "the weirdness of quantum mechanics, for so long the plaything of quirky science fiction, has found its technology (quantum computing), and is getting serious." This physics background makes *Proof of Concept* a work of "hard" science fiction – "meaning *solid*, solidly connected to real science, not fantasy" – rather than a merely "quirky" example of the genre (Jones 2018). The physics of *Proof of Concept* is a fictional extrapolation, of course – but arguably no more so than the novella's account of society and environment.

In any case, PSM draws upon actually existing quantum information theory, which parses quantum states in terms of information (qubits). The novella extrapolates this into the supposition that spacetime is computationally tractable – at least in principle, and using quantum rather than standard computation. PSM also draws upon the currently controversial theory of Bohmian mechanics, which claims to resolve the paradoxes of quantum uncertainty by giving a central role to nonlocality and entanglement. An isolated quantum system exists in a state of superposition, defined by a wave function: Schrödinger's cat is both alive and dead. Most interpretations of quantum mechanics state that the wave function collapses (the superposition breaks down) when the quantum system's isolation is breached: it is brought into contact with external forces. This is how a definitive outcome is determined: Schrödinger's cat is either dead or alive, but not both. But for Bohmian mechanics, very roughly, wave function collapse is never definitive. The quantum system's contact with external forces generates a new situation of entanglement and superposition, on a meta-level. Particular wave functions, associated with particular situations, collapse; but the wave function that defines the universe as a whole never does. The cat's individual fate is decided, but we are now entangled with it in a larger system, with its own wave function, and its own degrees of indeterminacy and superposition.

For Bohmian mechanics, everything in the universe is ultimately entangled with everything else. This is why quantum effects are nonlocal. As Jones puts it on her blog, all of reality "exists in superposition" – not just Schrödinger's alive-and-dead cat, but also "your own mind, the way you form your ideas and memories," and even "the galaxy" as a whole (Jones 2018). In the extrapolated physics of *Proof of Concept*, this is explicitly stated as a sort of koan: "something happening in a distant galaxy is affecting you ... right now. Everything is connected. There are no empty spaces and time does not pass."

According to PSM, if you could "track every live synapse in the information state of a moment of awareness," in all its confusions and superpositions, then you would reach an "integrated definition" of this state. The same applies to any other volume of space-time. Margrethe and her team are working, not with consciousness, but with what they call the Needle: a specially defined "volume of 4-D mapped information space." They seek to reach an integrated definition of this volume, using a "refraction technique" that gives them "nonspecific data." (The reason the data are "nonspecific" is that conventional, specific measurements would collapse the local wave function prematurely.) The "Proof of Concept" will be if they can "observe the integration state" of the qubits that make up the Needle, "including their instantaneous connections with the farthest distant quarters of the universe." Once this is accomplished, the connections can be activated: the scientists will be able to "shift this volume, quasi-instantaneously and with near-zero loss of integration, to some defined *elsewhere* in the local universe."

This is what Margrethe has touted to her financial backers as "the royal road to interstellar exploration": the principle behind the supposed starship that she has promised to build for the One Percent. Quantum entanglement is instantaneous; so "time is no object" and "neither is space." This means that, "if everything worked ... thousands of light-years could be crossed in a flash," without violating the relativistic speed limit. You cannot move faster than the speed of light; but Margrethe gets around this with a sort of sleight of hand:

In a sense, the Needle doesn't move at all. When it shifts, everything shifts with it: everything reforms, and it's somewhere else.

Nothing in particular actually moves in this scenario; rather, everything is rearranged, all at once. We know that "you can't get rid of travel time ... without cost"; but when everything is in superposition with everything else, the "cost" of shifting one volume of space-time is that other volumes get shifted as well. This is potentially quite ominous: if you "zoom off to your fourteen-thousand-light-years-from-home exoplanet," then "you cannot expect to find planet Earth exactly where you left it. Or looking the way you left it." The scientists cannot predict the scope of the changes that a shift will cause, for "the disturbance caused in information space by the shift swamped all measurement of the shift itself." The only thing they know for sure is that "size matters." They should be able to get away with shifting the Needle by itself, because "the 'volume' is tiny, our shift is infinitesimal." The changes will correspondingly be quite small. But shift anything larger – like an actual space-time volume the size of a starship – and the changes will be unpredictably disruptive. You can only shift a large volume "as long as you don't care what happens next."

I have no idea how plausible this actually is in scientific terms. But it exemplifies the way that *Proof of Concept* works as a narrative. Jones does not seek to resolve the contradictions that she observes, whether these be logical, social, intellectual, psychological, or narrative. Instead, she works through the ways that, on all of these levels, mutually incompatible tendencies nonetheless coexist, operating in superposition with one another. Unlike the MegaCorps, Jones relishes "fluidity, blur, and multiplicity." As Fredric Jameson has theorized, in science fictional extrapolation "heterogeneous or contradictory elements of the empirical real world are juxtaposed and recombined into piquant montages" (Jameson 2005, cited in Bould 2019).

Proof of Concept thus follows, in its own narrative development, the fictional scientific practice that it describes. In a first moment, the narrative holds a model state of superposed tendencies in isolation, in order to give it something like an integrated definition. The novella experiments, under controlled conditions, and from a distance, with certain tendencies and processes from the larger outside world in which it is set. But then, in a second moment, the narrative posits a shift. The integrated state emerges from isolation, and confronts the larger world from which it was derived. The model is now entangled with the very situation *of which* it is the model. Since everything is connected in superposition, this first shift leads to a cascade of other shifts – many of them disproportionately large.

This is why the action of *Proof of Concept* takes place at a considerable remove from the social world that the novella establishes so vividly. The story proper is set, far from the Hives and the Dead Zones, in a vast, newly discovered (and therefore still "pristine") underground cavern, known as the Giewont Abyss:

The deepest, largest terrestrial cavern in the world, far deeper than previous record holders, and hugely greater in volume ... The air was dry, cool, and very still ... It was an empty magma chamber, a scoured, flask-shaped hollow from which the molten rock had seeped, long ago ... a sunless, inside-out, unexplored alien planet.

The Giewont Abyss is an entirely isolated space: as close to an "alien planet" as you can find on the Earth itself. It is also nearly sterile and lifeless, with no organisms larger than bacteria. All this makes it an ideal place for scientific research. The Needle is insulated from all outside influences, placed in an "isolation chamber, sunk into bedrock and shielded above and below by trellised lines of force." Around it sits the Frame: "a closed-system lab facility, cold-sleep dorms, and living quarters ensemble." Once this physical structure has been built and staffed, everything is sealed off for a year, placed in "hard quarantine." Even GAM is denied access: there is "no mediation tracking ... *all contact with the world above severed.*" For the duration of the experiment, Margrethe and her team can work on their integrated definition of the Needle, while deferring any consideration of its entanglement with the greater world outside.

The Needle Voyager mission, as it is called, is a social experiment as well as a scientific one. Margrethe's group consists of 13 scientists; they are known as Needlers. But they are joined by 48 Tourists or LDMers: people from Dan Orsted's VLDMR crew. For once, these reality television stars will try to get along for a year in confined quarters, simulating the rigors of interstellar travel, without the continual surveillance of cameras and microphones, and without feedback from a global audience. The Frame is an entire self-sustaining microcosm: it includes, in addition to the labs and sleeping quarters, such "communal spaces" as "the oversize canteen, the games rooms, the gym, a strolling mall." There are even "vegetable gardens." Around it, the void of the Abyss stretches for miles.

The scientists and the LDMers initially view one another with distrust; the former mostly stick to their labs, while the latter "sprawled over ... the communal spaces," engaging in all sorts of "obnoxious" behavior. But eventually a kind of truce is reached. As we are told, in the narration's careful, wry, and semi-ironic manner, "mutual respect and cordial association broke out like a rash." After a while, they are socializing regularly, and even wildly partying together. The experiment seems to be a success: "Something human and untamed was happening ..."

The novella's protagonist, Kir, is "a scrawny, undersized young woman with wispy blond hair and yellowish-brown skin." She is a protégé of Margrethe, and part of the scientific team. Kir despises the Great Escape as media hype; and she detests the LDMers for promoting it. Why should we be "heading off to kill another living world," instead of tending to "the only world we have"? Kir has "fall[en] in love with the science" for its own sake; she really hopes that Margrethe will be able "to crack the deep code of Einstein's Universe (or Space-Time, or the 'whole multiverse,' or whatever you want to call it)." This is not a common attitude, when research can only be done if it is funded by the MegaCorps and the One Percent.

Kir has a different background from any of the other characters. Whereas they are all well-to-do hivizens, she was born and grew up in the Dead Zones. Thanks to this background, Kir is "lawless by nature ... a free spirit." Margrethe rescued Kir from the Zones, and adopted her – but at a price. When Kir was still a child, "way too young to give informed consent," computer hardware was embedded into her skull. Strictly speaking, "Margrethe had done nothing illegal" in performing this operation, since children from the Dead Zones don't have any legal rights in the first place. And in any case, "Kir now had a *much* better life" with Margrethe than she ever could have led in the Dead Zones. She still regards Margrethe with gratitude and awe, regarding her as both *"my father and my mother."* Kir also knows that Margrethe loves her back – at least to the limited extent that Margarethe is capable of loving anyone. But the bottom line is that Kir is still ultimately a "captive," bound both to Margrethe and to the "supercomputer in [her] head."

This device in Kir's head is a quantum computer, a *quaai* (quasi-autonomous artificial intelligence). It, or rather he, is named Altair. Although a quantum computer is genderless, Altair, like Da Jue, has arbitrarily been assigned masculine pronouns. Altair's relation to Kir seems more parasitic than symbiotic: Kir's "brain supplies [Altair's] life support ... If he wasn't hosted by a living human brain he'd be much more expensive and far too hot to run." And it seems likely that, in the long run, Altair's energy requirements will probably end up "shortening [Kir's] life." It is also troubling that the main reason for Kir's participation in the Needle Voyager mission is not on account of her own potential contributions, but because the project depends on quantum computation.

Though Kir and Altair are embodied together, they remain separate mental entities. Kir has no access to Altair's programs; often he operates entirely outside of her awareness. Altair, for his part, "is contained by ... firewalls, and blocked from access to [Kir's] personal thoughts." Nonetheless, in the course of the narrative, they start talking, and become something like friends. Kir hears Altair as a voice in her mind; and he understands when she verbally answers him. Altair seems to want to warn Kir about something that is going wrong with the mission; but he is constrained by his programming, and cannot tell her directly. As their relationship develops, Kir comes to realize that there is nothing "quasi" about Altair's intelligence; he is as fully sentient, with ideas and emotions, as any human being is. The trouble, as Altair bitterly puts it, is that Margrethe would "just rather not believe I'm a person." Kir and Altair find that what they have in common is that they are both Margrethe's prisoners: "*I am not free*, said Altair at last. *I am a slave. But neither are you free. Have you thought of that?*"

I will not go over the novella's plot in detail. Kir takes long walks through the Abyss outside of the compound, alone except for conversations with Altair. There is something beautiful about the total emptiness. Meanwhile, tension builds throughout the Frame. Despite the social disinhibition, things get more and more oppressive. People start dying. Three older scientists reject continuing life support, opting instead "not to delay [their] departure." People wonder why they came on the mission in the first place, if they knew that they could not last for a whole year. The contents of their minds are "harvested," or preserved in digital form, which raises all sorts of questions. Then Kir's boyfriend Bill, one of the LDMers, is murdered. Many people, both Needlers and LDMers, want to abort the mission; they are "frantic to escape." But they discover that there is no way to get out; it seems as if Margrethe and Dan are "determined to keep them prisoner."

The novella's ending comes as a brutal punch to the gut, even though it has been amply foreshadowed. We are given a retrospective explanation for everything that has happened. Dan and Margrethe appear to the crew in prerecorded "holopresence." They reveal that the Needle Voyager mission has already gone live. They are no longer on Earth. Instead of transporting just the Needle to a different space-time location, Margrethe and Dan have shifted the entire Frame along with it. Everyone else, and everything else, is gone. Dan announces that "Earth is sterilized of all human life." This may not literally be true, since "the consequences of a shift of this volume are unknowable." But major damage must have occurred. Earth is unquestionably no longer "where [Dan and Margrethe] left it, or looking the way [they] left it." If there are any survivors left on Earth, it will seem to them that

the installation in the Abyss has suffered something akin to a major, poisonous nuclear accident. Nobody will dare to approach for quite a while.

Proof of Concept, much like *Splendor and Misery*, ends with a leap into the unknown, judging that the old world is entirely irredeemable. The 55 remaining Needlers and the LDMers include "everyone [Margrethe] judged capable of starting again." They are all alone, ostensibly on their way to "a habitable world" somewhere else in the galaxy. These people are, for all intents and purposes, the "sole survivors" of a devastated Earth. They are being given a "second try"; Dan exhorts them to "do better" than human beings did the first time around.

Margrethe and Dan accept responsibility for the devastation they have caused. Their message to the crew is a posthumous one: "we have been capable of murder, and had to be erased. We are gone." Indeed, they have pushed things further than even the "the Extreme Population Control people" were willing to do. But at least they did not make an exemption for the superrich. Margrethe "took the One Percent's money and left them helpless on a foundering ship. That was the plan, always." The real horror of *Proof of Concept* is that its ending is something like the best-case possible outcome of unrestrained neoliberal governance. The One Percent are sending us to our doom; at least this way, they are made to suffer doom as well, instead of getting away with it all scot-free.

In spite of everything, Dan and Margrethe insist that their extreme action was justified:

> We simply saw that things were passing beyond the point of no return. We saw that the human species, though functionally extinct, could survive long enough to make the ruin complete. Earth had to be given back: before it was too late.

With their preemptive action, Dan and Margrethe have given the Earth back to its nonhuman inhabitants. The animals and plants will flourish amidst the radiation, the poisons, and the rubble. Margrethe explicitly compares the situation to that of Chernobyl: a historical reference for her, but a present-day actuality for us. She describes how, after the nuclear disaster, Chernobyl "became a wildlife refuge ... it's a story of hope." In the absence of human interference, "devastated ecologies can recover." From a nonhuman point of view, this seems to be true. Indeed, a 2019 study of Chernobyl revealed that "at present the area hosts great biodiversity ... All the studied groups maintain stable and viable populations" (Orizaola 2019).

Proof of Concept leaves the reader – leaves *me* – in a state of extreme shock, with little to palliate its troubling vision. In the time of capitalist realism, we tend to gravitate toward dystopias, because envisioning the end of the world is indeed the only way in which we are able to imagine that things could at least be *different*. In that sense, much recent dystopian fiction is actually sort of comforting. But Jones doesn't let us off the hook so easily; her vision is just too harsh and unrelenting. Recent dystopian fictions often feature, as their protagonist, a plucky young woman who manages to set things right. *Proof of Concept* nods to this formula, while undermining it. Kir is an extremely empathetic figure, but her powers of action are quite limited. Like all the others, she falls for the grand deception: "It was *Margrethe* who fooled me, because she had to fool everyone." The best that Kir can say, at the end of the novella, is that she and Altair are both finally "free" from Margrethe's domination. Altair agrees, telling her that he feels "okay ... apart from somewhat wishing I was dead." It is hard to feel any more hopeful than this, even if the Needle Voyager is a "lifeboat" thrown clear of the otherwise worldwide catastrophe.

Or perhaps there is something more. At one point in *Proof of Concept*, Kir has an odd vision, referring back to her childhood in the Dead Zones:

A tiny fish hung by a pseudo-rock in a poisoned stream. *How does it stay there, when the water's moving?* Kir the baby-scav couldn't make it out, and suddenly it – no, but something happened. Something had been poised, for an instant—

The vision only lasts for a moment. But Kir recalls it at the very end of the novella:

Call the truth a "philosophical koan" and you can play with the forbidden, the full impossible tumbling deck, the blur and multiplicity of reality, and who knows where that will end? Between banks of rusty rock in a contaminated stream, the tiny fish hangs suspended. Feelings, things, hurts, unassociated recall, cascading through the myriad dimensions. The fish thinks otherwise, but time is not a river.

Here we get all the states and moments in quantum superposition, and Kir remembers why she "[fell] in love with the science." In this extremity, we have at least recovered "the blur and multiplicity of reality" that is so hated by the MegaCorps. I do not think Jones is suggesting that this immanent mysticism can in any way compensate for all the horror and loss that the novella forces us to envision; if we revel in it, then we are deluding ourselves just as the fish does. But this suspension of "feelings, things, hurts, unassociated recall" may be the only thing we can cling to when – as the last sentence of *Proof of Concept* puts it – "all around them flowed the rushing dark."

Works Cited

afloweroutofstone. "Dialesbian Materialism." Tumblr. https://transbianlavender. tumblr.com/post/181476900484/afloweroutofstone-holy-shit-clippings. 2019.

Agamben, Giorgio. *Homo Sacer: Sovereign Power and Bare Life*. Trans. Daniel Heller Roazen. 1998.

Bachofen, Johan Jacob. *Myth, Religion, and Mother Right*. Trans. Ralph Manheim. [1861] 1992.

Barkow, Jerome, John Tooby, and Leda Cosmides, eds. *The Adapted Mind: Evolutionary Psychology and the Generation of Culture*. 1995.

Beckett, Chris. *Dark Eden*. 2012.

Beckett, Chris. *Daughter of Eden*. 2016.

Beckett, Chris. *Mother of Eden*. 2015.

Beckert, Sven and Seth Rockman, eds. *Slavery's Capitalism: A New History of American Economic Development*. 2016.

Bergson, Henri. *The Two Sources of Morality and Religion*. Trans. R. Ashley Audra, Cloudesley Brereton, and W. Horsfall Carter. 1935.

Blanchot, Maurice. "The Limit-Experience." In *The Infinite Conversation*. Trans. Susan Hanson, 202–229. 1993.

Boltanski, Luc and Eve Chiapello. *The New Spirit of Capitalism*. Trans. Gregory Elliott. New updated edition, 2018.

Bould, Mark. "Extrapolation." *Extrapolation*, 60(2): 98-99. 2019.

Burns, Todd L. "clipping. On Afrofuturism, Fast Rapping and Sound Design." *Red Bull Music Academy Daily*. https://daily.redbullmusicacademy.com/2016/09/clipping-interview. September 9, 2016.

Brassier, Ray. *Nihil Unbound: Enlightenment and Extinction*. 2007.

Brunner, John. *The Shockwave Rider*. 1975.

Canales, Jimena. *The Physicist and the Philosopher*. 2015.

Chalmers, David. "Facing Up to the Problem of Consciousness." *Journal of Consciousness Studies*, 2(3): 200–219. 1995.

Chuong, Edward B. "Retroviruses Facilitate the Rapid Evolution of the Mammalian Placenta." *Bioessays*, 35(10): 853–861. October 2013.

Chwistek, Leon. *The Limits of Science*. Trans. Helen Charlotte Brodie and Arthur P. Coleman. 1948.

clipping. Liner notes to *Splendor and Misery*. https://clppng.bandcamp.com/album/splendor-misery. 2016.

Conway, John H. and Kochen, Simon. "The Strong Free Will Theorem." *Notices of the AMS*, 56: 226–232. 2009.

Cooper, Melinda. *Family Values: Between Neoliberalism and the New Social Conservatism*. 2017.

Cooper, Melinda. "Turbulent Worlds." *Theory, Culture and Society*, 27(2–3): 167–190. 2010.

Davis, Mike and Daniel Bertrand Monk, eds. *Evil Paradises: Dreamworlds of Neoliberalism*. 2011.

Delany, Samuel R. *Stars in My Pocket Like Grains of Sand*. 1984.

Deleuze, Gilles. "Postscript on Control Societies," in *Negotiations*. Trans. Martin Joughin, 177–182. 1995.

Deleuze, Gilles. *Spinoza: Practical Philosophy*. Trans. Robert Hurley. 1988.

Derrida, Jacques. *Writing and Difference*. Trans. Alan Bass. 1978.

Dick, Kirby and Amy Ziering. *Derrida* (documentary film). 2002.

Edelman, Lee. *No Future: Queer Theory and the Death Drive*. 2004.

Engels, Friedrich. *The Origin of the Family, Private Property and the State*. Trans. Alick West. [1884] 1972.

Eshun, Kodwo. "Further Considerations on Afrofuturism." *CR: The New Centennial Review*, 3(2): 287–302. 2003.

Eshun, Kodwo. *More Brilliant Than the Sun: Adventures in Sonic Fiction*. 1998.

Ferdinand, Ruben. "A Little Analysis of clipping's Splendor & Misery." https://medium.com/@urbanfriendden/a-little-analysis-of-clipping-s-splendor-misery-2016-a4819ff92408. October 12, 2016.

Fisher, Mark. *Capitalist Realism: Is There No Alternative?* 2009.

Foucault, Michel. *The History of Sexuality Volume 1: An Introduction.* Trans. Robert Hurley. 1976.

Foucault, Michel. *The Order of Things: An Archaeology of the Human Sciences.* Trans. Alan Sheridan. 1994.

Foucault, Michel. *Security, Territory, Population: Lectures at the Collège de France, 1977–1978.* Trans. Graham Burchell. 2007.

Freud, Sigmund. *Beyond the Pleasure Principle and Other Writings.* Trans. John Reddick. 2003.

Friedman, Milton and Rose. *Free to Choose: A Personal Statement.* 1980.

Genius.com, Lyrics and commentary for Jay-Z, "Run This Town." https://genius.com/3574. 2009.

Genius.com, Lyrics and commentary for Lupe Fiasco, "All Black Everything." https://genius.com/Lupe-fiasco-all-black-everything-lyrics. 2011.

Goldschlager, Amy. Interview with Chris Beckett. *Kirkus Reviews.* www.kirkusreviews.com/features/chris-beckett/. April 2, 2014.

Gottleib, Anthony. "It Ain't Necessarily So." *The New Yorker.* www.newyorker.com/magazine/2012/09/17/it-aint-necessarily-so. September 10, 2012.

Grusin, Richard, ed. *The Nonhuman Turn.* 2015.

Halam, Ann. *Dr. Franklin's Island.* 2002.

Haraway, Donna. *Simians, Cyborgs, and Women: The Reinvention of Nature.* 1991.

Harman, Graham. *Immaterialism: Objects and Social Theory.* 2016.

Harman, Graham. "On the Horror of Phenomenology: Lovecraft and Husserl." *Collapse*, 4: 333–364. 2008.

Harman, Graham. *Weird Realism: Lovecraft and Philosophy.* 2012.

Harness, Charles L. "The New Reality." 1950. Collected in Charles L. Harness, *An Ornament to His Profession*, 1998.

Hopes, Addie. "Mermaid Marronage: Surviving the Plantationocene in *The New Moon's Arms.*" Conference presentation, Science Fiction Research Association, Milwaukee. 2018.

Hopkinson, Nalo. *Falling in Love With Hominids*. 2015.

Hopkinson, Nalo. *The New Moon's Arms*. 2007.

Hopkinson, Nalo. *Report from Planet Midnight*. 2012.

James, Robin. *Resilience and Melancholy: Pop Music, Feminism, Neoliberalism*. 2015.

Jameson, Fredric. *Archaeologies of the Future: The Desire Called Utopia and Other Science Fictions*. 2005.

Jameson, Fredric. *Postmodernism, Or, The Cultural Logic of Late Capitalism*. 1991.

Jemisin, N. K. "Summer Reading: Science Fiction." In *The New York Times Book Review*. www.nytimes.com/2014/06/01/books/review/jeff-vandermeers-authority-and-more.html. May 30, 2014.

Jones, Gwyneth. *Proof of Concept*. 2017.

Jones, Gwyneth. "*Proof of Concept* Acknowledgments Page." www.boldaslove.co.uk/blog/index.php?/archives/402-Proof-of-Concept-Acknowledgements-Page.html. April 9, 2017. (2017a).

Jones, Gwyneth. "UB#3: EUrovision Flash Mob, Proof Of Concept, & Movies." www.boldaslove.co.uk/blog/index.php?/archives/407-UB3-EUrovision-Flash-Mob,-Proof-Of-Concept,-Movies.html. February 12, 2018.

Kant, Immanuel. *Critique of Pure Reason*. Trans. Paul Guyer and Allen W. Wood. 1998.

Kant, Immanuel. *Critique of the Power of Judgment*. Trans. Paul Guyer and Eric Matthews. 2000.

Kincaid, Paul. "Proof of Concept by Gwyneth Jones." In *Strange Horizons* magazine. http://strangehorizons.com/non-fiction/proof-of-concept-by-gwyneth-jones/. May 15, 2017.

Kitcher, Phillip. *Vaulting Ambition: Sociobiology and the Quest for Human Nature*. 1985.

Knight, Nadine. "A Long Way Away: Unreachable Freedoms in Contemporary Afrofuturist Neo-Slave Narratives." *Journal of Science Fiction* 2(4): 26–44. December 2018.

Kuhn, Thomas. *The Structure of Scientific Revolutions*. 1962.

Kupermintz, Eden. "*prognotes – Clipping's Splendor & Misery." www.heavyblogis-heavy.com/2016/10/14/prognotes-clippings-splendor-misery-part-i-all-black-everything/. 2016.

Leary, John Patrick. *Keywords: The New Language of Capitalism*. 2018.

Lévi-Strauss, Claude. *Structural Anthropology*. Trans. Claire Jacobson and Brooke Grundfest Schoepf. 1963.

Levitt, Deborah. *The Animatic Apparatus: Animation, Vitality, and the Futures of the Image*. 2018.

Lovecraft, H. P. *Tales*. Ed. Peter Straub. 2005.

Marx, Karl. *Capital: A Critique of Political Economy*. Volume One. Trans. Ben Fowkes. 1976.

McBride, Rita and Glen Rubsamen, eds. *Futureways*. 2005.

McKittrick, Katherine and Sylvia Wynter. "Unparalleled Catastrophe for Our Species? Or, to Give Humanness a Different Future: Conversations." In Katherine McKittrick, ed., *Sylvia Wynter: On Being Human as Praxis*, 9-89. 2016.

McLuhan, Marshall. *Understanding Media: The Extensions of Man*. 1964/1994.

McLuhan, Marshall and Quentin Fiore. *The Medium is the Massage*. 1967.

Meillassoux, Quentin. *After Finitude: An Essay on the Necessity of Contingency*. Trans. Ray Brassier. 2008.

Mieillassoux, Quentin. "Iteration, Reiteration, Repetition: A Speculative Analysis of the Sign Devoid of Meaning." In Armen Avenessian and Suhail Malik, eds., *Genealogies of Speculation: Materialism and Subjectivity Since Structuralism*, 117-197. 2016.

Meillassoux, Quentin. *Science Fiction and Extro-Science Fiction*. Trans. Alyosha Edlebi. 2015.

Miévile, China. "Weird Fiction." In *The Routledge Companion to Science Fiction*, eds. Mark Bould, Andrew M. Butler, Adam Roberts, and Sherryl Vint, 510-515. 2009.

Merleau-Ponty, Maurice. *Phenomenology of Perception*. Trans. Donald A. Landes. 2012.

Morgan, Lewis Hentry. *Ancient Society*. 1877.

Morton, Timothy. *The Ecological Thought*. 2010.

Orizaola, Germán. "Chernobyl Has Become a Refuge for Wildlife 33 Years After the Nuclear Accident." www.pri.org/stories/2019-05-13/chernobyl-has-become-refuge-wildlife-33-years-after-nuclear-accident. May 13, 2019.

Pastuzyn, Ellisa D. et al. "The Neuronal Gene *Arc* Encodes a Repurposed Retrotransposon Gag Protein that Mediates Intercellular RNA Transfer." *Cell* 172: 275–288. January 11, 2018.

Pesic, Peter. "Wrestling with Proteus: Francis Bacon and the 'Torture' of Nature." *Isis* 90: 81–94. 1999.

Phillips, Rasheedah. *Black Quantum Futurism: Theory and Practice*. Volume 1. 2015.

PIAS. *clipping. Splendor and Misery*. http://mediapias.com/artistes/clipping-1. 2016.

Pinker, Steven. *The Blank Slate: The Modern Denial of Human Nature*. 2003.

Planck, Max. *Scientific Autobiography and Other Papers*, trans. F. Gaynor. 1949.

racked & dispatched. *Afro-Pessimism: An Introduction*. 2017.

Richardson, Robert C. *Evolutionary Psychology as Maladapted Psychology*. 2007.

Richman, Shaun. "Company Towns Are Still with Us." *The American Prospect*, http://prospect.org/article/company-towns-are-still-us. March 21, 2018.

Riskin, Jessica. *The Restless Clock: A History of the Centuries-Long Argument Over What Makes Living Things Tick*. Chicago, 2016.

Roberts, Adam. *The Thing Itself*. 2015.

Robinson, Kim Stanley. "Dystopias Now." In *Commune Magazine*. https://communemag.com/dystopias-now/. 2019.

Roosth, Sophia. *Synthetic: How Life Got Made*. 2017.

Rushkoff, Douglas. "Survival of the Richest." https://medium.com/s/futurehuman/survival-of-the-richest-9ef6cddd0cc1. July 5, 2018.

Schneider, Eric and Dorion Sagan. *Into the Cool: Energy Flow, Thermodynamics, and Life*. 2006.

Schrödinger, Erwin. *What Is Life?: The Physical Aspect of the Living Cell*. 1944.

Serres, Michel. *The Parasite*. Trans. Lawrence R. Schehr. 1982.

Shannon, Claude. *A Mathematical Theory of Communication*. 1949.

Shelley, Mary. *Frankenstein; or, The Modern Prometheus*. 1818.

Simak, Clifford D. *Out of Their Minds*. 1970.

Simak, Clifford D. "Shadow Show." 1953. Collected in Clifford D. Simak, *Strangers in the Universe*. 1956.

Straus, Matevž, and Razvan Zamfira. "Company Towns Are Back!" *Scenario Magazine.* www.scenariomagazine.com/company-towns-are-back/. October 4, 2017.

Taplin, Jonathan. *Move Fast and Break Things: How Facebook, Google, and Amazon Cornered Culture and Undermined Democracy.* 2017.

Thacker, Eugene. *After Life.* 2010.

Thomas, David Hurst. *Skull Wars: Kennewick Man, Archaeology, and The Battle For Native American Identity.* 2000.

Toffler, Alvin. *Future Shock.* 1970.

Tomlinson, Gary. *Culture and the Course of Human Evolution.* 2018.

u/opheres, "Re-translating the Air 'Em Out click track." *reddit.* www.reddit.com/r/ItsClippingBitch/comments/8p9c50/retranslating_the_air_em_out_click_track/. 2018.

Weinberg, Steven. *Dreams of a Final Theory.* 1993.

Wells, H. G. *The Island of Dr. Moreau.* 1896.

White, Caitlin. "Rapping In Space: How Clipping Broke The Fourth Wall And Entered The Fourth Dimension." *Uproxx.* https://uproxx.com/music/clippping-splendor-and-misery-daveed-diggs/. 2016.

Whitehead, Alfred North. *Process and Reality.* Corrected edition, ed. David Ray Griffin and Donald W. Sherburne. 1978.

Wikipedia. "Master/slave (technology)." 2017.

Wikipedia. "Timeline of computing 1950–79." 2008.

Woodard, Ben. "Dark Vitalism: Some Notes." *Naught Thought* blog. https://naughtthought.wordpress.com/2010/02/10/dark-vitalism-some-notes/. February 10, 2010.

Zebrowski, George. "Celebrating Charles L. Harness." In Charles L. Harness, *An Ornament to His Profession*, 1998.

Index